PERSONA AND SHAME

By the same author
A FILM TRILOGY
 (Through a Glass Darkly,
 The Communicants, [Winter Light],
 The Silence)

BERGMAN

PERSONA
and SHAME

The Screenplays of Ingmar Bergman

translated by Keith Bradfield

GROSSMAN PUBLISHERS · NEW YORK 1972

Persona and *The Snakeskin* originally published
in Sweden as *Persona* by
P.A. Norstedt & Soners förlag, Stockholm

Shame first published in this edition, 1972

© Ingmar Bergman, 1966, 1972
© This translation, Calder & Boyars Ltd, 1972

Published in 1972 in a hardbound and
paperbound edition by
Grossman Publishers
625 Madison Avenue, New York, N.Y. 10022
Reprinted 1974

SBN 670-15865-8 (hardbound)
      670-15866-6 (paperbound)

Library of Congress Catalog Card Number: 70-114948

Printed in Great Britain

Bound in U.S.A.

CONTENTS

THE SNAKESKIN

Written for the presentation of the
Erasmus Prize in Amsterdam, 1965

Artistic creativity has always manifested itself in me as a
sort of hunger. I have observed this need in myself with
some gratification, but I have never in all my conscious life
asked why this hunger should arise and demand to be
satisfied. In the last few years, as it has begun to ease off,
and been transformed into something else, I have begun to
feel it important to try to establish the reason for my
'artistic activity'.

I remember from very early childhood a need to show
what I had achieved; progress in drawing, the ability to
bounce a ball against the wall, my first strokes in the
water.

I remember feeling a great need to attract the attention
of the grown-ups to these manifestations of my presence in
the physical world. I never, it seemed to me, excited
enough interest in my fellow human beings. And so, when
reality no longer sufficed, I began to make things up,
regaling my contemporaries with tremendous stories of my
secret exploits. These were embarrasing lies, which inevit-
ably foundered on the scepticism of the world around me.
In the end I withdrew from fellowship and kept my
dreams to myself. A contact-seeking child, beset by
fantasies, I was quickly transformed into a hurt, cunning
and suspicious day-dreamer.

11

But a day-dreamer is not an artist other than in his dreams.

The need to get people to listen, to correspond, to live in the warmth of a fellowship, remained.

It became stronger and stronger as the prison walls of loneliness closed around me.

It was fairly obvious that the cinema should be my chosen means of expression. I made myself understood in a language that by-passed words, which I lacked; music, which I have never mastered; and painting, which left me unmoved. Suddenly, I had the possibility of corresponding with the world around me in a language that is literally spoken from soul to soul, in terms that avoid control by the intellect in a manner almost voluptuous.

I threw myself into my medium with all the dammed-up hunger of my childhood and for twenty years, in a sort of rage, I have communicated dreams, sensual experiences, fantasies, outbursts of madness, neuroses, the convulsions of faith, and downright lies. My hunger has been continuously renewed. Money, fame and success have been the astonishing, but basically unimportant, consequences of my advance. By this, I do not wish to discount whatever I may have achieved. I believe it has had, and perhaps still has, its importance. What is so comforting to me is that I can see what has passed in a new and less romantic light. Art as self-satisfaction can have its importance – particularly to the artist himself.

Today the situation is less complicated, less interesting, and above all less glamorous.

Now, to be completely honest, I regard art (and not only the art of the cinema) as lacking importance.

Literature, painting, music, the cinema, the theatre

beget and give birth to themselves. New mutations and combinations emerge and are destroyed; seen from the outside, the movement possesses a nervous vitality – the magnificent zeal of artists to project, for themselves and an increasingly distracted public, pictures of a world that no longer asks what they think or believe. On a few preserves artists are punished, art is regarded as dangerous and worth stifling or steering. By and large, however, art is free, shameless, irresponsible and, as I said, the movement is intense, almost feverish; it resembles, it seems to me, a snakeskin full of ants. The snake itself is long since dead, eaten out from within, deprived of its poison; but the skin moves, filled with busy life.

If I now observe that I happen to be one of these ants, then I must ask myself whether there is any reason to pursue the activity further. The answer is yes. Even though I regard the theatre as an old and well-beloved courtesan who has seen better days. Even though I, and many with me, find Westerns more stimulating than Antonioni or Bergman. Even though the new music gives us feelings of suffocation, from the mathematical thinning out of the air; even though painting and sculpture have been sterilized and waste away in paralysing freedom. Even though literature has been transformed into a mere cairn of words, with no message and no danger.

There are poets who never write, because they shape their lives as poems; actors who never perform, but who act out their lives as high drama. There are painters who never paint, because they close their eyes and conjure up the most superb works of art on the back of their eye-lids. There are film-makers who live their films and would never abuse their gift by materializing them in reality.

13

In the same way, I believe that people today can reject the theatre, since they live in the midst of a drama which is constantly exploding in local tragedy. They need no music, since their hearing is bombarded every minute by great hurricanes of sound, in which the pain barrier is both reached and surpassed. They need no poetry, since the new world philosophy has transformed them into creatures of function, bound to interesting – but poetically unusable – problems of metabolism.

Man (as I experience myself and the world around me) has set himself free, fearfully, breathtakingly free. Religion and art are kept alive for sentimental reasons, as a conventional courtesy to the past, or in benevolent concern for the increasingly nervous citizens of leisure.

I am still declaring my subjective view. I hope and am convinced that others have a more balanced and allegedly objective view. If now I take all these unfortunate factors into consideration and assert that in spite of everything I wish to continue making art, it is for one very simple reason. (I will disregard any purely material consider-ations).

This reason is *curiosity*. An unbounded, never satisfied, continuously renewed, unbearable curiosity, which drives me forward, never leaves me in peace, and completely replaces my past hunger for fellowship.

I feel like a prisoner who has served a long sentence and suddenly tumbled out into the booming, howling, snorting world outside. I am seized by an intractable curiosity. I note, I observe, I have my eyes with me, everything is unreal, fantastic, frightening, or ridiculous. I capture a flying particle of dust, perhaps it's a film – and of what importance will that be: none whatsoever, but I *myself* find it interesting, so it's a film. I revolve with the objects I have captured for myself and am cheerfully or melancholically occupied. I elbow my way in with the other ants, we do a colossal job. The snakeskin moves.

This and this only is *my* truth. I don't ask that it should be true for anyone else and, as comfort for eternity, it is naturally on the slim side. As a basis for artistic activity during the next few years it is entirely adequate, at least for me.

To be an artist for one's own sake is not always very agreeable. But it has one outstanding advantage: the artist is on an equal footing with every other creature who also exists solely for his own sake. Taken together, we are probably a fairly large brotherhood who exist in this way in selfish fellowship on the warm, dirty earth, under a cold and empty sky.

15

PERSONA

PERSONA is an AB Svensk Filmindustri film made in 1965, with the following cast:

ALMA	Bibi Andersson
ELISABETH VOGLER	Liv Ullmann
DOCTOR	Margaretha Krook
HERR VOGLER	Gunnar Björmstrand

The film was photographed by Sven Nykvist
The film was written and directed by Ingmar Begman

Persona

I have not produced a film script in the normal sense. What I have written seems more like the melody line of a piece of music, which I hope with the help of my colleagues to be able to orchestrate during production. On many points I am uncertain and at one point at least I know nothing at all. I discovered that the subject I had chosen was very large and that what I wrote or included in the final film (horrid thought) was bound to be entirely arbitrary. I therefore invite the imagination of the reader or spectator to dispose freely of the material that I have made available.

1

I imagine the transparent ribbon of film rushing through the projector. Washed clean of signs and pictures, it produces a flickering reflected light from the screen. From the loudspeakers we hear only the noise of the amplifier and the faint crackle of dust particles travelling through the playback head.

The light establishes itself and thickens. Incoherent sounds and short fragments of words, like sparks, begin to drip from the ceiling and walls.

From this whiteness emerges the contours of a cloud, no – a sheet of water, no – it must have been a cloud, no – a tree with a great leafy top, no – a lunar landscape.

The noise rises in coils, and whole words (incoherent and remote) begin to emerge like the shadows of fish in deep waters.

No cloud, no mountain, no tree burdened with foliage, but a face, its eyes locked into those of the spectator. The face of Sister Alma.

– Have you been in to Mrs Vogler, Sister Alma? No? Probably a good thing. We'll go in together. Then I can introduce you. Just let me tell you briefly about Mrs Vogler's situation and why you have been employed to look after her. Very simply – Mrs Vogler is an actress (as

23

you know) and was playing the last performance of *Electra*. In the second act she stopped speaking and looked around her in something like surprise. She wouldn't take a prompt or cue from the other actor, she just kept quiet for a minute. Then she went on playing, as if nothing had happened. After the performance she told the others she was sorry and explained her silence by saying simply: 'I got this terrible fit of laughter.'

— She took off her make-up and went home. She and her husband had a little supper in the kitchen. They chatted and Mrs Vogler mentioned what had happened at the performance, but in passing and with some embarrassment.

— Man and wife wished each other good night and retired to their bedrooms. The following morning they rang from the theatre and asked if Mrs Vogler had forgotten she had a rehearsal. The housekeeper went in to Mrs Vogler and found her still in bed. She was awake, but she didn't answer the housekeeper's questions and she didn't move.

— This state has now lasted for three months. She has been given every conceivable test. The result is clear enough. So far as we can see, Mrs Vogler is perfectly healthy, both mentally and physically. There is no suggestion of any hysterical reaction, even. In the course of her development as an artist and human being, Mrs Vogler has always been of a happy and realistic disposition and enjoyed excellent health. Is there anything you'd like to ask? In that case, we can go in to Mrs Vogler.

2

– Good morning, Mrs Vogler. I'm Sister Alma and I've been employed to look after you for a while.

Mrs Vogler watches her attentively.

— If you like, I'll tell you a bit about myself. I took my nursing certificate two years ago. I'm twenty-five years old and engaged. My parents have a farm in the country. My mother was also a nurse before she got married.

Mrs Vogler listens.

— Now I'll go and get your dinner tray. Fried liver and fruit salad. I thought it looked quite nice.

Mrs Vogler smiles.

— I'll just raise your pillows a little, so that you'll be comfortable.

3

— Well Sister, what do you think?

— I don't know, Doctor. It's difficult to say. I was looking at her eyes the whole time. First you think her face is so soft, almost childish, but then you look at her eyes and that's different. I don't know how to put it. She looks at you so severely, in a way. I wondered for a moment whether she didn't like me talking to her. Not that she seemed impatient at all. No, I don't know. Perhaps I should . . .

— Say what you were thinking, Sister.

— For a moment I thought I ought to refuse the job.

26

— Did something frighten you?

— No, I wouldn't say that. But perhaps Mrs Vogler should have a nurse who's older and more experienced, who knows more about life. I mean, I might not be able to manage her.

— How do you mean, manage?

— Mentally.

— Mentally?

— If Mrs Vogler's not moving is the result of a conscious decision, which it must be since she is perfectly healthy. . .

— Well?

— Then it's a decision that shows mental strength. I think whoever is going to look after her will need a lot of spiritual strength. I just don't know if I'm up to it.

— Sister Alma. When I needed someone to look after Mrs Vogler, I had a long talk with the matron at your school and she mentioned your name at once. She thought you were suitable in every way.

— I'll do my best.

4

Sister Alma has given Mrs Vogler her injection and helps arrange her pillows, puts out the bedside lamp, goes over to the window and pulls back the curtains. It is dusk, but the sky shines out over the heavy autumn tree-tops. Just above the cross on the window is a little reddish sickle of moon.

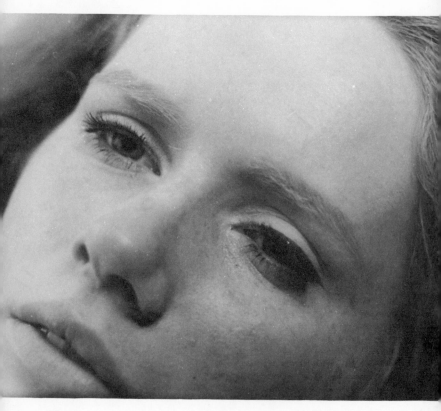

— I thought, Mrs Vogler, that you might like to lie and look at the twilight. I can pull the curtains a bit later on. Shall I turn the radio on for a bit, quietly? I think there's a play of some kind.

Sister Alma moves quickly, almost soundlessly, through the room, but she feels that Mrs Vogler is watching her the whole time. From the radio we hear an indescribable female voice.

— Forgive me, forgive me darling, you have to forgive me. All I want is your forgiveness. Forgive me so that I can breathe again — and live again.

The actress's diction is interrupted by Mrs Vogler's laugh, which is warm and hearty. She laughs until the tears come to her eyes. Then she grows quiet, in order to listen. The female voice continues indefatigably.

— What do you know of mercy, what do you know of a mother's suffering, the bleeding pain of a woman?

Mrs Vogler bursts out in another, equally cheerful, laugh. She raises her arm and takes Alma's hand, pulls her down by the bedside, fumbles with the volume control on the radio and the female voice swells to supernatural proportions.

— Oh God, God, somewhere out there in the darkness that surrounds us all. Look in mercy upon me. Thou who art love.

Sister Alma, in terror, turns off the radio and the steaming female voice. She looks with an uncertain smile at Mrs Vogler, whose forehead is wrinkled with quiet laughter. Mrs Vogler slowly shakes her head and placidly regards Sister Alma.

— No, Mrs Vogler, that sort of thing's beyond me. I like going to the theatre and cinema, but unfortunately I don't get round to it very often. I'm usually too tired by the evening. Though . . .

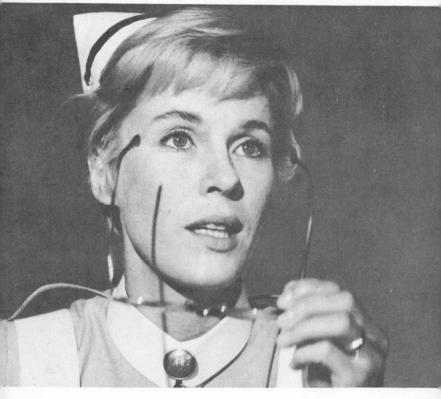

— Though I do have a tremendous admiration for artists and I think art is tremendously important in life — particularly for people who are in some kind of difficulty.

This last, Sister Alma says with some embarrassment. Mrs Vogler looks at her with attentive dark eyes.

— I don't think I'd better talk about these things when you're listening, Mrs Vogler. I'll be getting into deep waters.

— Shall I turn the radio on again? No? There might be some music. No music? Well good night, Mrs Vogler. Sleep well.

She releases the large, slightly moist hand with the high blue veins — a heavy, beautiful hand that seems older than the still young face. Then she leaves the room, we hear the two doors snap shut, the inner and the outer. We hear her say something in the corridor.

Finally, everything is quiet.

Elisabeth Vogler presses her head back against the hard pillow. Her injection is beginning to afford her a dozy sense of well-being. She listens in the silence to her own breathing and finds it alien but agreeable company. Tears well up in her eyes and run slowly to the sides over her temples down into the disarranged waves of hair. Her mouth is large, soft, half open.

It is growing dark. Trees dissolve and vanish as the sky

31

darkens. She hears remote, deep voices moving against her own calm respiration. Meaningless words, fragments of sentences, syllables, mixed together or dropping at even intervals.

Her eyes are still filled with tears.

5

Alma undresses.

Potters about her tiny room. Washes some stockings.

Waters a pining foliate plant of indeterminate species. Switches on the radio. Yawns a few times. Sits on the edge of the bed, in a pair of old pyjamas.

— You can go about almost any old way, do almost any old thing. I'll marry Karl-Henrik and we'll have a couple of kids that I'll bring up. That's all decided, it's in me somewhere. I don't have to work things out at all, how they're going to be. That makes you feel very safe. And I'm doing a job I like. That's a good thing too — only in a different way. I wonder what's really wrong with Mrs Vogler.

6

One morning a few days later, Sister Alma finds her patient in a state of marked anxiety. On the coverlet lies an unopened letter.

— Would you like me to open the letter, Mrs Vogler?

Affirmative

— Do you want me to read it?

New affirmative

— Shall I read it out to you?

Sister Alma has already learned to understand and inter-pret Mrs Vogler's facial expressions and she seldom guesses wrong. She opens the letter and begins to read, in a voice that she tries to make as impersonal as possible. From time to time she hesitates, the writing being very difficult to read. Certain words she cannot make out at all.

The Letter

Dearest Elisabeth. Since I am not allowed to see you, I am writing. If you don't want to read my letter, then don't. In any case I cannot help seeking this contact with you, since I am plagued by continual anxiety and the constant question: have I done you harm in some way? Have I hurt you without knowing it? Has there been some frightful misunderstanding between us? I ask myself a thousand questions and get no answer.

As far as I know, we were happy recently. Surely we have never been so close to each other. Do you remember saying: I'm only just beginning to understand what marriage really means. You have taught me (I can't read what it says) you have taught me (it's impossible to read) you have taught me that (now I get it) we must look upon each other as two anxious children full of good will and the best of intentions, but governed (it must be governed) by forces that we do not entirely control.

Do you remember saying all that? We were out walking together in the woods and you stopped and caught on to my belt.

*Sister Alma breaks off and looks at Mrs Vogler in dismay.
She is sitting up in bed, her face distorted.*

— Shall I go on?

Shakes her head

— You'd better lie down again, Mrs Vogler. Shall I get you
something soothing?

As before

— No? Oh, there was a photo in the letter. A photo of
your boy. Would you like it? He looks awfully nice.

*Mrs Vogler takes the photo and looks at it for a long time.
Sister Alma stands by the edge of the bed, her hands
resting against the end. She has put the letter away in her
apron pocket. Mrs Vogler tears the picture down the
middle, regards the pieces with disgust and hands them to
Sister Alma.*

*That same evening Sister Alma visits a little local cinema,
which is showing a film several years old with Elisabeth
Vogler in the main part.*

8

*The same evening as Sister Alma's visit to the cinema an
episode occurs that is worth noting. Mrs Vogler (like many
of the other patients here) has a television set in her room.
To many people's surprise, Mrs Vogler displays a great*

35

interest in the most varied types of programme. What she tends to avoid is television theatre.

This evening she sees a political feature programme. It includes a scene showing a Buddhist monk who burns himself to death in the street in protest against the government's religious policy. Watching this scene, Mrs Vogler begins to scream loudly and piercingly.

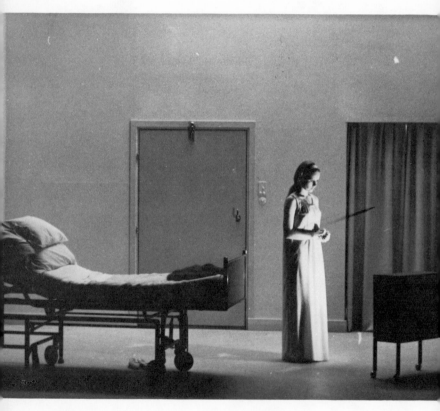

9

The woman doctor comes in to Mrs Vogler's room and sits down in the visitor's chair.

— Elisabeth, there's no real point in you staying at the hospital any more. I think it's only doing you harm. If you

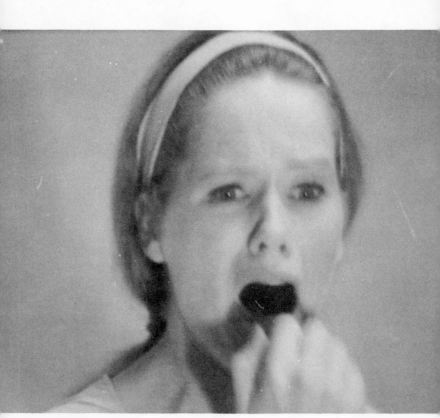

don't want to go home, I suggest that you and Sister Alma move out to my summer place by the sea. There's no one around for miles. The countryside is a great healer, I promise you.

She sits for a while thinking, drawing her nails along the inside of her hand. Mrs Vogler is resting on the bed, in a dove-grey dressing-gown that reaches her ankles. She is peeling a pear with a sharp little silver knife. The juice is

38

running over her fingers.

— Well, what do you think?

Mrs Vogler looks at her with an apologetic smile. The doctor's expression remains as demanding as before.

— You might as well make up your mind at once, otherwise you'll only worry yourself to death thinking about it. I've already spoken to Sister Alma. She wasn't terribly keen, because she has some sort of boy-friend. But when I said he could live in the guest cabin on his free days, she gave in. Also, we can bribe Sister Alma. I imagine she's saving up for a trousseau or something equally conservative and unpleasant.

Mrs Vogler eats a slice of the over-ripe pear. She keeps her fingers spread wide, finds a paper napkin and dries her hands and mouth carefully, then wipes the handle of the knife.

— Sister Alma is a great little person. She'll do you a world of good.

The doctor gets up from her chair, goes over to the bed, pats Mrs Vogler's foot.

— It doesn't matter. Let me know tomorrow or the day after. You'd better have something to torture yourself with, now everything else has been taken away.

At this point, Mrs Vogler really does look tortured.

— Now you *look* really tortured! The main thing is to touch the pain nerve carefully.

Mrs Vogler shakes her head.

— We have to touch it, you know. Otherwise it only gets worse.

Mrs Vogler screws up her eyes as if to shut the doctor out, then looks up again cautiously. The doctor is still there.

— I do understand, you know. The hopeless dream of *being*. Not doing, just being. Aware and watchful every second. And at the same time the abyss between what you are for others and what you are for yourself. The feeling of dizziness and the continual burning need to be unmasked. At last to be seen through, reduced, perhaps extinguished. Every tone of voice a lie, an act of treason. Every gesture false. Every smile a grimace. The role of wife, the role of friend, the roles of mother and mistress, which is worst? Which has tortured you most? Playing the actress with the interesting face? Keeping all the pieces together with an iron hand and getting them to fit? Where did it break? Where did you fail? Was it the role of mother that finally did it? It certainly wasn't your role as *Electra*. That gave you a rest. She actually got you to hold out a while more. She was an excuse for the more perfunctory performances you gave in your other roles, your 'real-life roles'. But when *Electra* was over, you had nothing left to hide behind, nothing to keep you going. No excuses. And so you were left with your demand for truth and your disgust. Kill yourself? No — too nasty, not to be done. But you could be immobile. You can keep quiet. Then at least you're not lying. You can cut yourself off, close yourself in. Then you don't have to play a part, put on a face, make false gestures. Or so you think. But reality plays tricks on you. Your hiding place isn't watertight enough. Life starts leaking in everywhere. And you're forced to react. No one asks whether its genuine or not, whether you're true or false. It's only in the theatre that's an important question.

41

Hardly even there, for that matter. Elisabeth, I understand that you're keeping quiet, not moving, that you have put this lack of will into a fantastic system. I understand it and admire you for it. I think you should keep playing this part until you've lost interest in it. When you've played it to the end, you can drop it as you drop your other parts.

10

Inexorably, the ribbon of film rattles through the projector. It travels at considerable speed. 24 frames a second. 27 long metres a minute. The shadows run over the white wall. Magic, of course. But unusually sober and merciless magic. Nothing can be changed, undone. It all thunders forth again and again, always with the same cold, immutable willingness. Put a red glass in front of a, lens, the shadows turn red – but what does it help? Load the film upside-down or back-to-front, the result will not be very different.

There is only **one** *radical change. Turn off the switch, extinguish the hissing arc, rewind the film, put it in its case and forget it.*

11

At the end of the summer, Mrs Vogler and Sister Alma move out to the doctor's summer house. It lies out of the way, with a long strip of shore facing the open sea to the north and a steep rocky bay to the west. Behind the house

extend a heath and a patch of woodland.

Mrs Vogler's stay by the sea does her good. The apathy that crippled her while in hospital begins to retire in the face of long walks, fishing trips, cooking, letter-writing and other diversions. At times, however, she sinks back into a vast melancholy, a petrified pain. At such times she becomes immobile, lethargic, almost extinguished.

43

Sister Alma enjoys her rural seclusion and devotes the utmost care to her patient. Her attention never fails and she sends long and detailed reports to the doctor.

12
An Episode

They are sitting together at the great white garden table.

Sister Alma is cleaning fungi and Mrs Vogler has a fungus chart in front of her, trying to classify the unusual ones. They sit beside each other in the sun and wind. It is afternoon. The sea shivers and throws sparks.

Mrs Vogler seizes Alma's wrist and studies the inside of her hand, placing her own beside it, comparing.

Alma pulls back her hand with a laugh.

— It's unlucky to compare hands, didn't you know?

13
Another Episode

A calm day, with the intense light of high summer. They have taken the motorboat out to sea, turned off the motor and lain down to sunbathe, each with a book. Alma

breaks the silence and attracts Mrs Vogler's attention:

— May I read you something from my book? Or am I disturbing you? It says here: 'All this anxiety we bear with us, our disappointed dreams, the inexplicable cruelty, our terror at the thought of extinction, the painful insight we have into the conditions of life on earth, have slowly crystallized out our hope of heavenly salvation. The great shout of our faith and doubt against the darkness and silence is the most terrifying evidence of our forlornness, our terrified unexpressed knowledge.'

14

It is early morning and the rain is rattling on the windows. Heavy storm clouds pile up and the sea roars among the rocks in the bay.

The two women are sitting together at the window table, manicuring their hands.

— People should do things about themselves. I don't think I would be any less ordinary, if I changed. But there's a lot about myself I don't like.

She looks quickly at Elisabeth, who is busy with the nail of her ring-finger.

— Well, of course, I really like my job. Even when I was little, I never thought of being anything else. Really, I'd like to work in the operating theatre. That's awfully

47

interesting. I'm starting a course this spring.

She interupts herself. This cannot be of any interest. But she notices that Elisabeth Vogler is looking at her attentively. She becomes slightly embarrassed, but gains courage.

— Doing something about yourself. The worst thing about me is I'm so lazy. It gives me a bad conscience, I'm so lazy. Karl-Henrik is always on at me, saying I haven't got any ambition. He says I live like a sleep walker. I don't think that's fair, though. I had the best marks in my group in the exam. But I suppose he means something else.

She smiles, and leans over the table for the coffee thermos. Pours coffee for Mrs Vogler and herself.

— Do you know what I really want? At the hospital where I trained they have a home for old nurses. People who have been nurses all their lives, just living for their work. They've always worn their uniforms. They live there in their little rooms, they live and die near their hospital. Imagine believing in something so much that you devote your whole life to it.

She drinks some of the strong, black coffee.

Mrs Vogler sits leaning slightly forward, with her arms on the table. Her gaze is fixed unblinkingly on Alma's face. To Alma this is fascinating, disturbing.

— Having something to believe in. Doing something,

thinking your life has a meaning. That's the sort of thing I like. To hold on tight to something, whatever happens. I think people ought to. And mean something to other people. Don't you think so?

— I know it sounds childish. But I believe in it. If you don't . . . You have to *know*. Particularly if you don't have a religion.

She changes her tone of voice, smooths the hair up from her forehead and leans backwards in the chair, looking out through the window. Thinking approximately: I don't care what that actress is sitting there thinking. Of course, she doesn't think the way I do.

— Goodness, what a storm.

Later in the day. The rain and the storm have eased off slightly. The two women have eaten lunch and are sitting on high stools on either side of the bar counter fixed to the wall.

— He was married. We had an affair for five years. Then he got tired of it. But I was terribly in love. I really was. He was the first, too. I *remember* it all as absolute agony. Long periods of agony and then short times when —

She doesn't know what word to use. She smokes nervously, a little unused to it.

— It just reminded me, now that you have taught me to smoke. He smoked constantly. Thinking about it after-

49

wards, like this, I suppose it was all very dreary. You know, like a novelette, only real.

She looks hesitantly at Elisabeth, who is smoking calmly. Waiting and listening.

— In some way, it was never quite real. I don't know how to explain. At least, *I* was never quite real to *him*. What I went through was real enough. It really was. But in a way, I thought it all belonged, in some nasty way. That was the way it was. *Even the things we said to each other.*

Afternoon. Heavy, grey, humid stillness, with only the sound of the breakers and dripping roofs and trees. Somewhere a window is open and lets in a cold fragrance of salt and seaweed, wet wood and rain-drenched juniper bushes. They have lit a fire in the open fireplace in the bedroom and curled up in Elisabeth's bed with blankets around their legs. They each have a glass of sherry within reach. Alma has drunk quite a lot. Elisabeth Vogler is still extremely attentive. Listening to each tone of voice, noting every movement. Alma becomes increasingly unself-conscious, unaware, fascinated and confused that someone (for the first time in her life) should be interested just in her. She talks faster and faster.

— A lot of people have said I'm a good listener. That's funny, isn't it? I mean, no one's ever bothered to listen to me. I mean, like you are doing now, you are listening to me now. And you look kind. I think you're the first person who's ever listened to me. And it can't be particularly interesting, can it? And yet there you sit. You

50

could be reading a good book instead. Goodness, how I'm going on. I hope it doesn't bore you. It's so nice to talk.

Elisabeth Vogler shakes her head and smiles softly, her cheeks have grown slightly red.

— No, everything feels so warm and nice just now, I feel it and I've never felt like this in all my life.

She stops talking and laughs. Elisabeth laughs with her and caresses her cheek very gently like a sister. Alma drinks up the contents of her glass.

— I've always wanted a sister, but all I have is a whole crowd of brothers. Seven of them. Funny, isn't it? And I was the last of the litter. I've always had boys of all ages around me, ever since I can remember. But it's been fun. I like boys.

She becomes secretive, bursting with a desire to tell. Secret marvels.

— You know all about that, of course, from your own experience. You're an actress and you've been through so much. You do know, don't you?

Elisabeth Vogler looks at her in astonishment.

— I like Karl-Henrik a lot and — well, you know, maybe you only fall in love once. But I am faithful to him, of course. Otherwise in our job there are other . . . possibilities, I can tell you. It wasn't that.

She thinks it over a bit more, pours out more sherry for herself and Elisabeth, leans back against the wall and sighs, wipes the hair from her forehead.

— It was last summer. Karl-Henrik and I went on holiday together. It was in June and we were quite alone. He went into town one day and it was sunny and hot, so I went down to the water. There was another girl there, sunbathing. She lived on an island nearby and had taken the canoe over to our beach because it lay to the south and was much more private, you see.

Elisabeth sees and nods. Alma notes this fact with a rapid, almost shamed smile. Puts her glass down on the bed-side table. Again, she wipes a non-existent lock of hair from her forehead.

— We lay there sunbathing quite naked and slept for a bit

53

and woke up and put on some oil. We each had a big straw hat over our faces, you know, one of those big cheap ones. I had a blue ribbon round mine. Sometimes I peeped through the hat at the scenery and the sea and sun. It was all so funny. Then I saw two figures jumping on some of the rocks high above us. Now and then they hid themselves and peeked at us from behind the stones. 'There's a couple of boys looking at us,' I said to the girl. Katarina, she was called. 'Let them look,' she said, and turned over on her back. It was such a strange feeling. All the time I wanted to get up and put on my bathing robe, but I lay there on my stomach with my bottom in the air not at all embarrassed, all sort of calm.

The whole time I had Katarina beside me with her little breasts and thick thighs and great bush of hair. She lay absolutely still, just giggling a bit. I saw the boys coming closer. Now they didn't worry at all. They stood there looking at us, without trying to hide. They were both awfully young, about sixteen I should think.

Alma lights a cigarette. Her hand is shaking and she almost gulps for breath. Elisabeth Vogler remains completely immobile, almost obliterated. When Alma offers her a cigarette, she simply shakes her head.

— One of the boys, who had a bit more courage, came up and squatted down beside Katarina. He pretended to be busy with his foot, sitting there poking between his toes. I began to feel all wet, but I lay still on my stomach with my arms under my head and the hat over my face. Then I heard Katarina say: 'Why don't you come here a bit.' And she took the boy's hand and pulled him over to her and

54

helped him off with his jeans and shirt.

Suddenly he was over her, and she was helping him and holding her hands round his thin, hard bottom. The other boy sat up on the slope, staring. Katarina laughed and muttered something in the boy's ear. I saw his red face, sort of swollen next to me. Then I turned and suddenly said: 'Why not come to me too?' And Katarina laughed and said: 'Off you go to her now.' And he pulled himself out of her and fell over me, all hard, and took hold of one of my breasts so that I shouted because it hurt, and I was all ready somehow and came almost at once, can you believe it? I was just going to say be careful, so that I don't get a baby, when he came too, and I felt it, I've never felt it in all my life before or since, how he shot it into me. He held my shoulders tight and bent backwards, and it felt as if it was never going to end. And it was all hot, and came again and again. Katarina lay on her side looking at us, holding her hand round his balls from behind, and when he was finished she took him in her arms and made herself come with his hand. And when she came, she screamed like anything. Then we started laughing, all three of us, and called for the other boy, whose name was Peter. He came slowly down the slope, looking all confused and frozen in the sunshine. He can only have been about thirteen or fourteen, we saw, when he came up. Katarina unbuttoned his trousers and played with him, he sat there all serious and quiet while she stroked him and took him in her mouth. Then he began to kiss her on the back and she turned to him and took his head between her hands and gave him her breasts. The other boy got so excited that he and I started again. It went very fast and it was as good for me as the first time. Then we had a swim and then we left

55

each other. When I came home, Karl-Henrik was already back from town. We had dinner and drank some wine that he had bought. Then we went to bed. It's never been so good between us, before or since . . .

Evening. The rain and storm have stopped. The ground-swell moves down on the rocky beach. Otherwise every-thing is quiet. The lighthouse is on, swinging its arc of light over the heath.

— Then I got pregnant, of course. Karl-Henrik, who is studying medicine, took me to a friend of his who did an abortion on me. We were both pretty happy to get away with it that easily. We didn't want any children. Not just then, anyway.

Suddenly Alma begins to cry. A confused sobbing, filled with pleasure. Elisabeth Vogler lays her broad hand over Alma's. Alma sighs, tries to speak, but abandons any idea of finding words.

— It doesn't fit, nothing hangs together when you start to think. And all that bad conscience for things that don't matter. You understand what I mean? Can you be quite different people, all next to each other, at the same time? And then what happens to everything you believe in? Isn't it important at all? Oh, it's all so silly. No reason to start howling, anyway. Wait a minute, I must blow my nose.

She blows her nose, dries her eyes, looks around and gives a little artificial laugh.

— It's night already. Just imagine my going on like that. I've been talking about myself all day and you listened. What a bore for you. My life can't be of any interest to you. People should be like you.

Elisabeth gives a surprised smile. Alma clears her throat. She finds it very difficult to collect her thoughts. Also, she is extremely tired and excited.

— That evening when I had been to see your film, I stood

57

in front of the mirror and thought 'We're quite alike.' (*Laughs*) Don't get me wrong. You are much more beautiful. But in some way we're alike. I think I could turn myself into you. If I really tried. I mean inside. Don't you think so?

She devotes a little confused reflection to this idea. Then, rather sulkily and miserably:

— And you wouldn't have any difficulty, of course, turning into me. You could do it just like that. Of course, your soul would stick out a bit everywhere, it's too big to be inside me. It would look all sort of odd.

Alma lays her heavy head on the table and pushes her arms out over its top. She closes her eyes and yawns.

—You'd better get off to bed, otherwise you'll fall asleep at the table, *says Mrs Vogler in a calm, clear voice.*

Alma fails at first to react, but then she slowly realizes that Elisabeth is speaking to her. She sits up and stares out to sea, unable to say a word.

— Yes, I'll go to bed now. Otherwise I'm sure to fall asleep at the table. It wouldn't be very comfortable.

15

That night Alma has a strange experience. She has slept very soundly for a few hours, but is woken up by an overfull bladder. Day is beginning to break and the sea-birds are screaming to high heaven down in the bay. She pads out onto the porch, round the corner and disappears behind some juniper bushes. There she squats down and urinates for a long time with pleasure, still more asleep than awake. Coming in, she shivers with cold for a while and feels slightly unwell. Soon, however, she is overwhelmed by a new drowsiness.

She is woken up by someone moving in the room. A white

figure gliding soundlessly to and fro by the door. At first she is afraid, but soon realises that it is Elisabeth who has come in to her.

For some reason, Alma fails to say anything. She lies there immobile, with half-closed eyes. After a moment Elisabeth, who is dressed in a long-white nightdress and a little crocheted cardigan, comes over to her bed. She bends down over Alma. Caresses her cheek with her lips. Her long

hair falls forward over her forehead and encloses their faces.

16

The following morning they are taking up nets together, something they both enjoy.

— Elisabeth . . .

— ?

— I'd like to ask you something. Did you talk to me last night?

Elisabeth smiles and shakes her head.

—Where you in my room last night?

Still smiling, she shakes her head again. Alma bends deep down over the net.

17

Sister Alma drives the ancient car carefully along a winding, bumpy forest road. She is going down to the post-office in the village with some letters. One of them is from Mrs Vogler to the doctor. It lies on the top of the heap in the front seat, the back of the envelope upwards.

Alma sees that it has not been sealed. She turns the car into a little side road and stops, finds her glasses in her handbag and opens the letter.

The Letter

My dear, This is how I should always like to live. Keeping silent, living in isolation, cutting down one's needs, feeling how one's battered soul finally begins to straighten out. I am beginning to get back elementary but forgotten sensations, things like a ravenous hunger before dinner, a childish drowsiness in the evenings, curiosity in a fat spider, the joy of going barefoot. I am blank and obstinate. Floating as it were in a mild semi-slumber. I am aware of a new health, a sort of barbaric cheerfulness. Surrounded by the sea, I am cradled like a foetus in the womb. No, no longing, not even for my little boy. But of course, I know he is all right and that makes me calm.

63

Alma is good, a real diversion. She takes care of me, spoils me in the most touching way. She has a robust, earthy sensuality that pleases me. She moves with a self-evident ease, which is both stimulating and relaxing. Of course, her very physical nature is part of my security. I think she is happy enough and she is rather attached to me, actually a little in love, in an unconscious and charming way. It's extremely amusing to study her. She's rather 'knowing', has a lot of opinions on morals and life, she's even a bit

bigoted. I encourage her to talk, it's very educational. Sometimes she weeps for past sins (some sort of episodic orgy with a completely strange teenager, plus subsequent abortion). She complains that her ideas about life fail to fit her actions.

Anyway I have her confidence and she tells me her troubles large and small. As you see, I am grabbing all I can get and as long as she doesn't notice it won't matter . . .

Alma has been reading slowly, jerkily, with long pauses. She has got out of the car, walked a few paces, sat down on a stone, got up again.

Such treachery.

She comes back late saying that the car broke down on the road and she had to go to a garage.

18

An autumn morning, with clear air and the warmth of summer. A strong light on the stones of the terrace and the rough gravel of the path. Sister Alma wakes up early as usual (her room faces east). She goes to the kitchen, squeezes herself a glass of orange juice, takes the glass in her right hand and pads out barefoot into the brilliant sunlight. She seats herself on the lowest step of the porch and drinks the juice slowly, screwing up her eyes as she looks out over the dazzling mirror of water.

She puts her empty glass down beside her, then knocks it over as she looks for her sun glasses in the pocket of her bath-robe. Splinters of glass lie spread over the steps and the gravel.

She stiffens, in a gesture of annoyance. Then rises muttering to herself, gets a brush and pan, carefully sweeps up all the broken glass, meticulously and laboriously. She squats down, picks glass with her fingers, looks carefully around her, it all seems to be gone, empties the pan into the trash can. Returns to the steps, lights a cigarette, observes the insect life on the gravel path through her sun glasses.

Suddenly she sees a large, irregularly shaped piece of glass shining among the stones on the path. A piece from the bottom of the glass, with a jagged rising edge. She reaches for it, then stops her hand in mid-movement.

She hears Mrs Vogler moving in the house.

After a moment's thought she gets a magazine, puts on her wooden shoes and opens out one of the reclining chairs on the terrace. The spear edge of the glass is a few yards to her right, glimpsed to one side of the tinted lens. She flips through her magazine, which is greasy from sun-tan lotion and contains colour supplements.

Elisabeth Vogler emerges onto the steps with her little coffee tray. She is wearing a short jacket over her bathing suit and is bare-legged, barefoot. She puts the tray down on a garden table and moves across the gravel in various directions, first to get a deck-chair, then to lean a rake against the wall.

Every now and again her feet come close to the spear of glass.

Then she lies back with her coffee and her book. Everything goes quiet.

Sister Alma gets up and goes to her room to put on her bathing suit.

When she comes out again, Elisabeth Vogler is standing crouched forward on the step, pulling the piece of glass from the arch of her left foot. The blood wells up from the clean-cut wound.

Sister Alma stands absolutely still for a moment taking in the scene, meets Mrs Vogler's look without blinking.

19

A cold, sunny morning. Elisabeth Vogler walks through the various rooms, looking for Sister Alma. Who is not there. She goes down to where they bathe. No one there. She goes up to the garage. The car is standing there. The trees creak and complain, the shadows of clouds fly over the moss. The wind is from the north, and the breakers roar down in the bay.

When she returns to the terrace Alma is there, standing with her back against the wall, looking out over the sea.

Elisabeth comes up to her. Alma turns her face, she is wearing sun glasses.

— Have you seen my new sun glasses? I got them in the village yesterday.

Elisabeth goes into the house, looks for her cardigan and her book. Comes out again. As she walks past Alma, she caresses her cheek, very lightly. Alma lets it happen, leaning back still against the wall. Elisabeth sits down in the big wicker chair.

71

— I see you're reading a play. I'll tell the doctor. It's a good sign.

Elisabeth looks up at Alma, enquiringly. Then she returns to her reading.

— Perhaps we can leave this place soon. I am beginning to miss town. Aren't you, Elisabeth?

Elisabeth shakes her head.

— Would you do something for me? I know it's asking a lot, but I could do with your help.

Elisabeth looks up from her book. She has been listening to Alma's tone of voice and, for a moment, there is a trace of fear in her eyes.

— It's nothing dangerous. But I do wish you would *talk to me*. I don't mean anything special. We could talk about the weather, for instance. Or what we're going to have for dinner, or whether the water's going to be cold after the storm. Cold enough to stop us going in. Can't we talk for a few minutes? Or just for a minute? Or you read me something from your book. Just say a couple of words.

Alma is still standing with her back to the wall, her head leaned forward, the black sun glasses on her nose.

— It's not easy to live with someone who doesn't say anything, I promise you. It spoils everything. I can't bear to hear Karl-Henrik's voice on the telephone. He sounds so artificial. I can't talk to him any more, it's so unnatural. You hear your own voice too and *no one else!* And you think 'Don't I sound false'. All these words I'm using. Look, now I'm talking to you, I can't stop, but I hate talking because I still can't say what I want. But you've made things simple for yourself, you just shut up. No, I must try not to get angry. You don't say anything, that's your business, I know. But just now I *need* you to talk to me. Please please, can't you talk to me, just a bit! It's

73

almost unbearable.

A long pause. Elisabeth shakes her head. Alma smiles, as if she were trying not to cry.

— I knew you'd say no. Because you can't know how I feel. I always thought that great artists had this tremendous feeling of sympathy for other people. That . . . they created out of sympathy with people, from a need to help them. Silly of me.

She takes off her glasses and puts them in her pocket. Elisabeth sits there, anxious and immobile.

— Use it and throw it away. You've used me — I don't know what for — and now you don't need me anymore you're throwing me away.

Alma is about to go into the house, but stops on the threshold, and gives a subdued howl of desperation.

— Yes, I know, I can hear perfectly well how artificial it sounds. 'You don't need me any more and you're throwing me away.' That's what's happened to me. Every word. And these glasses!

She takes her glasses from her pocket and throws them down on the terrace. Then she sinks down onto the steps.

— No, I'm just hurt, that's all. I'm out of my mind with misery and disappointment. You've done me such harm. You laughed at me behind my back. You're a devil, an absolute devil. People like you ought to be shot. You're mad. Just think, I read that letter of yours to the doctor, where you laugh at me. Just imagine, I did that, it was still open and I've got it here, I never sent it and I promise you I've really read it. And you got me to talk. You got me to tell you things that I've never said to any one. And you just pass it on. What a case history for you. Isn't it? You can't do it — you can't!

She suddenly comes up, grabs Elisabeth's arms and starts shaking her.

– Now you're going to talk. Have you anything – now, my God, I'm going to make you talk to me!

With surprising strength, Elisabeth tears herself free and hits Alma in the face with the back of her hand. The blow is powerful enough for Alma to stumble and almost fall.

76

But she quickly regains her balance, rushes at Elisabeth and spits in her face. Elisabeth hits her again, this time over the mouth. She at once begins to bleed. Alma looks round. She sees a thermos on the table, she seizes it, pulls out the stopper and hurls the boiling hot water at Elisabeth.

— No, stop it! *(Screams Elisabeth, crouching down out of the way.)*

Alma stops, her fury is transformed, she stands there a moment or two looking at Elisabeth, who has bent down to pick up the broken pieces of thermos. Alma is bleeding from the nose and mouth. She wipes her hand over her face, she looks terrible.

— Well at least you were frightened. Weren't you? For a few seconds you may have been absolutely honest. An honest fear of death. Alma's gone mad, you thought. What sort of a person are you, really? Or did you only think 'I'll remember that face. That expression. That tone of voice'. I'll give you something you won't forget.

She suddenly whips out her hand and claws Elisabeth's face. Then something astonishing happens. The actress begins to laugh.

— That's right. Laugh. Things aren't that simple for me. Not that funny either. But you always have your laugh.

She goes into the bathroom, runs cold water over her mouth and nose. After a while, the flow of blood almost stops. She stuffs a little wad of cotton-wool in her nose. Combs her hair and feels deathly tired, yawns again and again.
When she emerges, Elisabeth is standing in the middle of the kitchen floor, drinking coffee from a large cup. She offers it to Alma, who greedily gulps some of it down. Then the two women begin to occupy themselves with various jobs in the kitchen.

Alma stops Elisabeth as she is passing, taking her wrist.

78

— Does it have to be like this? Is it so *important* not to lie, always to tell the truth, always to have the right tone of voice? Is it necessary? Can you even live without talking as it comes? Talking nonsense, excusing yourself, lying, evading things? I know you have stopped talking because you're tired of all your parts, all the parts you could play perfectly. But isn't it better to let yourself be silly and sloppy and lying and just babble on? Don't you think

you'd be a bit better really, if you let yourself be what you are?

Elisabeth smiles, ironically.

— No. You don't even understand what I mean. Someone like you is impossible to get at. The doctor said you were mentally healthy. I wonder if your madness isn't worse than anything else. You're *playing* healthy. And you do it so well that everyone believes you. Everyone except me. Because I know just how rotten you are.

Alma goes out from the kitchen onto the terrace. The sun is now directly to the south and shines into her eyes, which are smarting with tears. She smokes a cigarette and shivers in the clear, cold afternoon.

— What am I doing? *(She whispers to herself.)*

She sees Elisabeth walking towards the beach, with long, controlled strides. She throws away her cigarette and treads on it. Calls 'Elisabeth, wait!' and runs after her, catches her up, walks along by her side.

— Elisabeth, forgive me, if you can. I'm behaving like a fool. I mean, I'm here to help you. I can't understand what got into me. You made me behave like an idiot. You must forgive me. But it was that awful letter. Only when I think about it, I could have written just as bad a letter about you. But I felt so disappointed. And you asked me to talk about myself. And I'd had a lot to drink and you were so kind, so kind and understanding, and it was great to have a

chance to talk about it all. And I suppose I was a bit
flattered too, a great actress like you taking an interest in
me. I think I almost hoped you would have some use for
what I told you. People are funny, aren't they? It's sheer
exhibitionism. Only it isn't that I wanted to say. Elisabeth,
you have to forgive me anyway. Because I like you so
much and you've meant so much to me. You've taught me
so much and now I don't want us to be enemies. You see?

*Alma stops in order to attract Elisabeth's attention, but
she walks on unconcernedly and vanishes among the rocks
on the shore. Alma screams after her, furiously.*

— No, you don't want to forgive me. You won't forgive
me. You're proud, aren't you? You won't stoop to my
level, because you don't have to. I'm not going — I'm not
going to!

*She is shouting furiously, hears her own voice, the
unctuous mortification in it, and groans weakly, painfully.
She sits down on a stone and lets the cold wind blow
through her soul, lets herself be filled with the heaviness of
the sea.*

20

Alma returns to the house.

*It is already dusk, the sun has set in a thick mist and the
sea has grown quiet. A cold fog rolls in over the coast.
Fog-horns in the distance.*

She bears inside her a rough desire for vengeance and a powerless anxiety; she feels listless, slightly sick, and goes to bed without eating.

After a few hours of heavy sleep, she is awakened by a feeling of paralysis – a stiffness seeking its way in towards her lungs and groping at her heart. The fog rolls in through the open window and the room floats in a grey half-light.

She succeeds in raising her hand to the bedside lamp – but no light comes.

The little transistor radio is scraping and gurgling to itself. A faint voice is heard from a distance.

– don't speak, don't listen, cannot comprehend – What means are we – us to persuade – to listen. Practically – excluded. These continuous calls upon –

The voice is drowned in powerful disturbance. Then silence, and only the fog-horns can be heard, infinitely far away.

Suddenly, someone is calling. The voice is that of a man. He is shouting, 'Elisabeth!'.

Alma manages to get out onto the floor, shut the window, walk along the corridor into Elisabeth's room.

Here she finds the same grey, indeterminate half-light.

Elisabeth is lying on her back in bed. Her face is pale and she has dark circles under her eyes. Her breathing is hardly noticeable. Her mouth is half-open, like that of someone dead.

Alma bends over her, feels her neck and forehead and takes her pulse. It is weak but regular.

She moves her mouth so close to Elisabeth's face that her lips can feel the breath of the sleeping woman. Cautiously, she touches her chin and closes her mouth.

— When you're asleep your face is all slack and your mouth is swollen and ugly. You've got a nasty wrinkle across your forehead, too Soon you won't have any secrets left. Your eyes aren't shining any more — now you're just a helpless, exposed lump of meat. You smell of sleep and crying and I can see the pulse in your neck. You've got a little scar there too, from an operation, which you cover up with make-up. Now he's shouting again out there. I'll go and find out what he wants with us. Away out here in our loneliness.

Alma leaves the sleeping woman and wanders from one room to the other, looking. She comes to the back of the house. To the garden.

She hears someone talking behind her back and turns round with a feeling of bad conscience. She sees a heavily built man of about fifty. He gives her an embarrassed smile.

— I'm sorry if I frightened you.

— I'm not Elisabeth.

Alma glimpses a figure behind the man's back, Mrs Vogler, who is watching her with a faint, ironic smile.

— The absolute limit of pain . . . my letters . . . All these words . . . *I'm* not making any demands . . .

The man is still embarrassed. Alma experiences a crawling sense of anguish at this humiliating piece of striptease. The whole time, Mrs Vogler's secret smile is there in the shadows. The man puts his hand over her shoulder.

— I didn't want to disturb you, don't think I don't understand. The doctor explained a number of things to me. (*He gives a melancholy smile.*) The most difficult thing is to explain to — your little boy. But I'm doing what I can. There's something deeper there, that it's difficult to see.

He looks at her with an uncertain, yielding look. The narrow mouth twitches. He is collecting his courage.

— You love someone, or rather you say that you love someone. It's something you can take hold of, comprehensible like words. I mean . . .

— Mr Vogler, I am not your wife.

— And so you are loved. You form a little community. This gives security, you see a possible way of enduring, don't you. Oh! How can I say everything I thought without getting lost, without boring you?

84

*The whole time Alma can see Mrs Vogler's face, her smile.
And Alma hears herself speaking with artificial tenderness.*

— I love you as much as before.

— I believe you.

*The man's eyes fill with tears, his mouth is very close to
hers.*

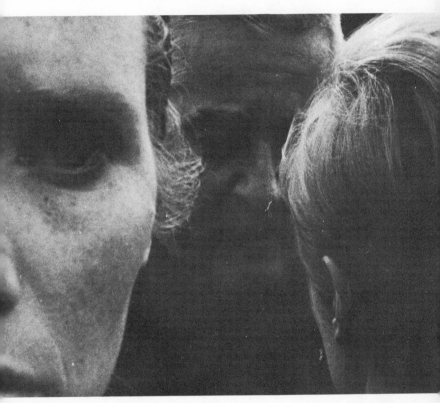

— I have believed so much, every time as whole-heartedly, as childishly. People seek each other, try to comprehend each other, try to leave themselves behind.

But Alma protects herself with her artificial voice.

— Don't worry so, my darling. We have each other. We have faith in each other. We know each other's thoughts, we love each other. That's true. Isn't it?

Mrs Vogler's face has grown serious, almost numb with averted pain. But Mr Vogler goes on.

— To understand each other as children. Hurt, helpless, lonely children. And the important thing is the effort, isn't it? Not what we achieve.

He becomes silent and dries his eyes with a shy movement of his hand. Alma makes an ultimate effort. Her voice is forced, false.

— Tell our little boy that Mummy will soon be back, that she has been sick and is longing to see him. Don't forget to buy something for him. It's to be a present from Mummy, don't forget.

— You know I feel such a tenderness towards you, Elisabeth. It's difficult to bear, almost. I don't know what to do with my tenderness.

Alma answers in a jarring tone of voice.

— I live from your tenderness.

Behind the man's back, Elisabeth Vogler makes a grimace of disgust. Now he leans over Alma and kisses her on the mouth, strokes her breasts and mutters caressing, appealing words. Alma lets it all happen, looking the whole time into Mrs Vogler's large eyes.

The ultimate point of suffering has not yet been reached:

— Do you like being with me? Is it good with me?

— You're a wonderful lover, darling. You know that, my love.

— My darling. Elisabeth, darling.

Now she can no longer endure, it breaks and she whispers, her face close to his, her forehead against his hairy ear:

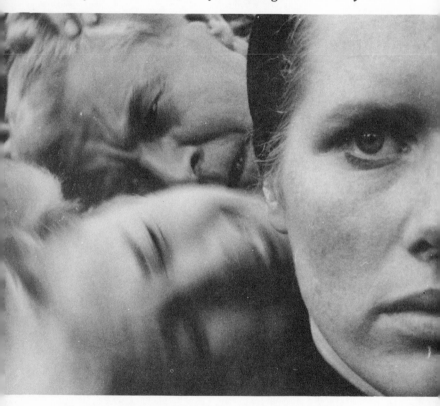

— Give me something to stupefy my senses, or beat me to death, kill me, I can't do it any longer, I can't. You mustn't touch me, it's shame, a dishonour, it's all counterfeit, a lie. Just leave me alone, I'm poisonous, bad, cold, rotten. Why can't I be allowed just to die away, I haven't the courage.

All this in a fairly controlled voice. Mrs Vogler, behind her husband's back, turns away with an expression of boredom.

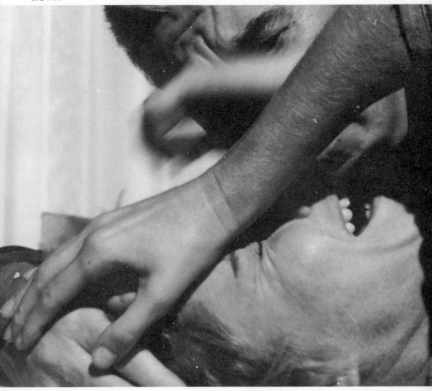

Mr Vogler takes Alma in his arms and holds her close to him, comforting her. His hand touches her forehead, her shoulder, squeezes her clenched fist. In a hoarse, desperate voice, he mutters and mumbles meaningless words that have lost any truth. Tearless, with smarting eyes, he stares at her alien mouth.

Mrs Vogler turns her face to the spectators out there in the darkness, speaking with a rough, almost raucous voice.

— Words like emptiness, loneliness, strangeness, pain and helplessness have lost their meaning.

21

Alma is alone, her pulse is beating faster. She turns back towards the house, enters a room that she has never seen, a sort of built-in glass verandah with a sleepy paraffin lamp in the ceiling. In the middle of the room is a large table. At the table sits Elisabeth Vogler, dressed in Alma's uniform.

Alma goes up to the table, and sits down opposite her. After a long silence, Alma begins to speak.

— Now I've learned quite a lot.

— learned quite a lot. (*Says Mrs Vogler.*)

Alma places her right hand on the table and turns the palm upwards. Elisabeth watches attentively, then raises her left hand, places it on the table and turns the palm upwards.

This procedure is repeated several times, the tension steadily increasing. Alma has tears in her eyes, but manages to control herself.

— Let's see how long I can manage. (*She says aloud.*)

— long I can manage. (*Answers Mrs Vogler.*)

Alma claws at her bare arm with her nails. A narrow streak of blood appears. Elisabeth leans forward and takes up the blood between her lips. Alma buries her hand in Elisabeth's thick hair and holds her face pressed tightly against her arm. She has to lean far over the table.

— I'll never be like you. (*She whispers quickly.*) I change the whole time. There's nothing definite, everything moves the whole time, *you can do what you like.* You'll never reach me.

And when Elisabeth pulls loose and throws her head back, Alma blows up her cheeks like a child blowing a balloon and then lets the air leak out between her lips with a faint bubbling noise. Elisabeth shakes her head in terror but then puts out her tongue with an expression of scornful cruelty.

Unable to think of anything else to do, they sit watching each other with bored faces and sullen lips.

Then Alma sees that Elisabeth Vogler is pulling herself together for a violent effort. She moves her mouth as if she were speaking and slowly words force their way from her throat. Only the voice is still not hers, nor Alma's, but a weak and anxious voice, uncontrolled and unclear.

— Perhaps a form of trespass, a shade of despair. Or the other, counselling, and it all gathers. No, not inwards. It ought to, but that's where I am. Yes, then you could cry, or cut up your leg.

The voice grows fainter still. Elisabeth Vogler sways, as if

92

she were going to fall down against the table, onto the floor, but Alma seizes her hands and holds them fast.

— The colours, the sudden swing, the incomprehensible disgust at pain and then all the many words. I, me, we, us, no, what is it, where is closest, where can I get a grip?

Alma holds her hands fast, looking into the eyes. The whole time she is shivering, she feels grey and shrivelled. The elderly whining voice continues to rise, becomes shrill and disagreeable.

— The failure that never happened when it should, but which came unexpectedly at other times and without warning. No, no, now it's another sort of light, which cuts and cuts, no one can protect themselves.

Alma presses her breast against the table. Mrs Vogler breaks off her piping monologue and raises her eyes, looks at Alma's torn, ruined face and frozen, contracted shoulders, and makes a violent movement to free herself, as if she were chained fast to a corpse; but Alma holds her tightly, firmly over her wrists.

22

At this point the projector should stop. The film, happily, would break, or someone lower the curtain by mistake; or perhaps there could be a short circuit, so that all the lights in the cinema went out. Only this is not how it is. I think the shadows would continue their game, even if some

93

happy interruption cut short our discomfort. Perhaps they no longer need the assistance of the apparatus, the projector, the film, or the sound track. They reach out towards our senses, deep inside the retina, or into the finest recesses of the ear. Is this the case? Or do I simply imagine that these shadows possess a power, that their rage survives without the help of the picture frames, this abominably accurate march of twenty-four pictures a second, twenty-seven metres a minute.

Now Alma sees:

Under Mrs Vogler's right palm lies a photograph. Alma lifts away her hand. The picture, torn in two, is of Elisabeth's four-year-old son. A soft, hesitant, child face, a small skinny body, on long skinny legs.

The two women stare at the photograph for some time. Then Alma begins to speak, slowly, groping for words.

— Nothing could be more difficult, could it?

Elisabeth shakes her head.

— But shall we talk about it?

Affirmative from Elisabeth.

— One evening at a party. It was late and pretty noisy. Sometime in the early morning someone said 'Elisabeth Vogler has practically everything she needs as a woman and an artist.' 'And what's missing?' I asked. 'You're not

94

motherly.' I laughed, because I thought the whole idea was ridiculous. But after a while I found myself thinking about it every now and again. I got more and more worried and then I let my husband give me a child. I wanted to be a mother.

A long pause. The torn photograph lies on the table. The paraffin lamp flickers and the shadows in the room start to move. Alma continues.

— So Elisabeth Vogler the actress got pregnant. When I realized I couldn't change my mind, I got frightened. Didn't I?

Elisabeth inclines her head.

— frightened of the responsibility, of being tied down, frightened of drifting away from the theatre, frightened of the pain, frightened of dying, frightened of my body swelling up. But the whole time I played the part . . .

Elisabeth turns her eyes away.

— the part of a happy young expectant mother. And everyone said: 'Isn't she beautiful now she's pregnant. She's never been so beautiful.'

Elisabeth tries to say something, but fails.

— In the meantime you tried several times by yourself to abort. And you failed. In the end you went to a doctor. He realized it was no longer possible. When I saw there was no

95

way out, I became ill and began to hate the baby and wished for it to be still-born.

— It was a long and difficult delivery, I was in agony for days. In the end, the baby was pulled out with forceps. Elisabeth Vogler looked with disgust and terror at her crippled, piping baby. Left alone with her first-born, she kept hoping and muttering:

— Can't you die now, can't you die.

— and I thought what it would be like to kill the baby, smother it under the pillow as if by accident, or crack its head against the radiator. But he survived.

Elisabeth Vogler leans her head against her hands and is shaken by quiet sobs. Alma sits in the same way, speaking inwardly. The photograph of the soft, hesitant child's face lies untouched.

— The child survived as if to spite me and I was forced to hold this repulsive, shaking creature to my breasts, which ached and pained from the milk which refused to come. I got boils, my nipples broke and bled — it was all a long, humiliating hallucination. The child was sick. It cried unceasingly, day and night, I hated it, I was afraid, I had a bad conscience.

— Finally the boy was taken care of by a nurse and relations and Elisabeth Vogler was allowed to get up from her sick-bed and return to the theatre.

The photograph: the peering suspicious eyes, the taut skinny neck, one shoulder slightly hunched up, questioning, doubting. Alma goes on:

— But the suffering was not over. The little boy had an incredible, violent love for his mother. I protect myself, defend myself desperately, because I know I cannot repay it. I feel it every day. It hurts so terribly, so terribly. The agony of my conscience never leaves me. And so I try and try. But it leads only to clumsy, cruel encounters between me and the boy. I can't, I can't, I'm cold and indifferent, and he looks at me and loves me and is so soft I want to hit him, because he won't leave me alone. I find him disgusting with his thick mouth and ugly body and wet appealing eyes. I think he's disgusting and I'm afraid.

Alma hears this voice, speaking on and on through her own mouth, and she stops and tries to avoid Elisabeth's eyes. Then she speaks very quickly.

— I don't feel like you, I don't think like you, I'm not you, I'm only trying to help you, I'm Sister Alma. I'm not Elisabeth Vogler. It's you who are Elisabeth Vogler. I would very much like to have — I love — I haven't —

Alma stops, sees herself for a brief moment, this is Alma, this is Elisabeth and herself. She can no longer distinguish, nor does it matter. Elisabeth laughs, shortly, coarsely.

— Try to listen. (*Whispers Alma.*) Please. Can't you hear what I'm saying? Try to answer now.

Elisabeth lifts her face from her hands. It is naked, sweating. She nods, slowly.

— Nothing, nothing, no, nothing.

— Nothing.

— It'll be alright. That's how it must be.

98

Elisabeth Vogler lets her head fall back again. Alma releases her hands. She sinks further. Alma carries her hand to her parched lips.

Then darkness.

24

The doctor is sitting behind her desk, mildly triumphant. She turns directly to the audience.

— Early in December Elisabeth Vogler returned to her home and to the theatre, both of which welcomed her with open arms. I was convinced all along that she would go back. Her silence was a role like any other. After a while she no longer needed it and so she left it. It is difficult, of course, to analyse her innermost motives. With such a complicated mental life as Mrs Vogler's. But I would put my money on strongly developed infantility. And then of course all the rest: imagination, sensitivity, perhaps even real intelligence. (*Laughs.*) Personally I would say you have to be fairly infantile to cope with being an artist in an age like ours.

The doctor is very pleased with what she has said, particularly the last bit.

25

A grey twilight with soft falling snow and a dark uneasy sea.

Alma moves in a great stillness.

One day a man comes with a motor-saw and an axe. The silence is shattered by the furious screaming as he cuts through the trunks. Alma offers him food and coffee. They exchange a few amicably indifferent words.

Alma has plenty to do, in her thoughts and with her hands. She says to herself.

— Day after day I go here, trying to write a letter. I know that it will never be written. Yesterday I cleaned out your desk. I found a photograph there. A little boy of about seven. He is dressed in a cap, short trousers, stockings and a nice little overcoat. His face is pale with fear and his eyes are black and wide. He is holding his arms high above his head. Behind him, on one side, are men and women with great bundles, staring numbly at the camera. On the other side are some soldiers in steel helmets and heavy boots. The soldier nearest the boy has his rifle at the ready, pointing at the boy's back. Autumn leaves are piling up in the gutter.

Alma moves through the dim rooms, among covered furniture and rolled-up carpets. She stops by one of the big windows and sees the man and his horse down on the terrace. The snow is falling in great white flakes.

— I really do like people a lot. Mostly when they are sick and I can help them. I'm going to marry and have children. I think that is what is going to happen to me here in life.

100

Alma's little conversation is interrupted by Mrs Vogler's face, filling the picture. A howling wide-open face, distorted by terror, with wild wide-open eyes and furrows of sweat running through her theatre make-up.

The picture grows white, grey, the face is wiped out. Is transformed into Alma's face, starts to move, assumes strange contours. The words become meaningless, running and jumping, finally vanishing altogether.

The screen flickers, white and silent. Then darkness – letters flutter over the picture, the end of the film running through the aperture.

The projector stops, the arc lamp is extinguished, the amplifier switched off. The film is taken out and packed into its brown carton.

SHAME

SHAME is an AB Svensk Filmindustri film, made in 1967, with the following cast:

EVA	Liv Ullmann
JAN	Max von Sydow
JACOBI	Gunnar Björnstrand
MRS. JACOBI	Birgitta Valberg
PHILIP	Siggi Fürst
LOBELIUS	Hans Alfredson
OSWALD	Ingvar Kjellson
INTERROGATION OFFICER	Frank Sundström
DOCTOR	Ulf Johanson
ROUND-SHOULDERED BLOND MAN	Frej Lindqvist
FAT MAN	Rune Lindström
ELDER OFFICER	Willy Peters
CONDEMNED MAN	Ake Jörnfalk
GUARD	Bengt Eklund
INTERVIEWER	Vilgot Sjöman
JOHAN	Björn Thambert
SECRETARY	Karl-Axel Forsberg
A LADY IN THE INTERROGATION ROOM	Brita Oberg
PRIEST	Gösta Prüzelius

SHOPKEEPER'S WIFE   Agda Helin
FEMALE PRISON WARDER   Ellika Mann

The film was photographed by Sven Nykvist
The film was written and directed by Ingmar Bergman

1

Scene: a somewhat tumbledown two-storey house at the edge of the woods. White plaster. A few greenhouses, a plot of garden. Some ancient fruit trees. In the yard is a large Ford, which has seen better days. To the right of the house an outside privy, tool-shed, a chicken yard and some rabbit cages.

The house is surrounded by a stone wall, parts of which have fallen down. The road follows the wall, then swings off towards the sandy hills and the sea.

A morning in late summer. Stillness. Far off, the sound of the sea. A moulting old dachshund dozing in the sun. Some hens on the porch. A fat cat hunts voles under the wall.

Inside the house, an alarm clock rings.

Eva and Jan Rosenberg are asleep in a large iron bed. He is a lean, longish man of about forty, with a sensitive face, downy sun-bleached hair and anxious eyes.

Mrs Rosenberg is younger, but thin and angular. A round childish face, wide-open eyes and a determined chin. Her thick hair has been braided tightly together for the night. She sleeps in the plainest of white shifts, the man is wearing faded, ragged pyjamas. The sun shines in through a tattered blind. A few large flies are buzzing against the windows.

When the alarm rings, they both wake up. Eva gets out of bed at once and goes down to the kitchen to make breakfast. The man sits for a long while on the edge of the bed, leaning forward, regarding his toes. He yawns, scratches his chest.

Having lit a fire in the stove, Eva returns to the bedroom and begins splashing about with water. Rather noisily. She washes the entire upper part of her body with a large cloth, then cleans her teeth. Jan watches the procedure without enthusiasm. Eva starts to do her hair, loosening the braid and combing with long, powerful strokes. She has put on a cardigan and a pair of worn trousers.

JAN: I had the weirdest dream. Do you know what I dreamed?

Eva does not answer.

JAN: I dreamed we were back in the orchestra, sitting beside each other rehearsing the Fourth Brandenburg Concerto, the slow movement. It was in the morning, the floor of the platform smelled of fresh varnish. Dorati was conducting. And everything that's happening now – it was all behind us. We remembered it like a terrible dream, and we were grateful to be back. I woke up crying – can you imagine? I started crying even when we were playing – it was the slow movement, you know the one . . .

He hums a few bars.

EVA: Aren't you going to shave today either?
JAN *(sadly):* Yes, all right. If you really want me to.

Eva puts up her hair and returns to the kitchen. Jan eases his feet into his old slippers, gives a depressed little sigh. Pulls on his clothes.

Eva pours a greenish drink into their cups.
On the table is a plate of zwieback and some boiled eggs.

JAN: I couldn't get this damned herb tea down at all. Now I actually quite like it. Why are you in a bad mood?

EVA: I'm not in a bad mood.

JAN: You're in a very bad mood. You always are these days. It's as if everything was my fault somehow.

EVA: Please Jan, hurry up and eat. We've got to go to the mayor with the strawberries, I promised them by nine o'clock.

JAN: If we get any money today, we might buy a bottle of wine.

Eva suddenly smiles; Jan takes her hand and kisses it quickly on the inside.

JAN: I think I'm getting a wisdom tooth. Do you think the dentist is still in town? We can look, anyway, can't we. When we've delivered the strawberries, I mean. Wisdom teeth can be very nasty. I had one once up here on the right and the doctor had to pick it out bit by bit. It was a real operation, it took several hours. Without any anaesthetic. I was down for a couple of weeks with a fever afterwards. The scar still aches when the weather changes. I only hope this one isn't as bad. That would be marvellous, wouldn't it? Will you look and see if it's swollen? Eva, please. Have a look, love. Can you see anything?

Eva looks. She can't see anything. Or perhaps she hasn't

bothered to look properly.
They have come out of the house. The old dachshund
wakes up, wags his tail violently and runs across their feet.
Eva is wearing black clogs, Jan a pair of worn sandals.

EVA: Did you pay the telephone bill?
JAN: Oh God, I forgot. Anyway, what's the point of
    paying for something we haven't got. The darned thing
    never works.

110

EVA: You know we have to have the telephone.

JAN: All right. Yes, I know. But we don't get all that many orders.

EVA: We've got to have the telephone. Otherwise we might as well pack up.

JAN: Anything you say.

Jan disappears into the greenhouse. Eva goes to the chicken run. The dachshund follows them both at once, wandering from one to the other, his nose to the ground and his tail curled attentively.

Eva finds some new-laid eggs and Jan gets together the boxes of strawberries, which have stood in the greenhouse overnight.

Far away we hear the sound of church bells.

JAN: Eva! Can you hear the bells? Is today a holiday or something? It's an ordinary Friday, isn't it? I don't like the sound of church bells on a week-day. What does it mean?

EVA: Nothing. Hurry up, now. We're already late.

JAN: What's the time?

EVA: Half past seven. Twenty-five to, actually.

They pack the cartons of strawberries into large bags and put them in the boot of the Ford. Jan pours petrol in from a can. Eva picks up a coat from the house, locks the door and puts the key under the doorstep. They get into the car. The old dachshund climbs up into the back seat. The cat pads over the gravel path. A wind blows along the edge of the woods, which darken from the shadows of clouds.

EVA: I think it's clouding over. Shouldn't you take your

111

leather jacket? In case it rains.

Jan gets out, finds the key under the step, unlocks the door and is gone. Eva waits for a while in the car. After a few minutes, she grows impatient.
She finds him upstairs, sitting in a chair by the wall. His face is turned away. The leather jacket lies in a heap on the floor.

EVA: What is it now?

Jan has obviously been crying. He doesn't answer, just shakes his head and gets up. As he passes Eva in the doorway, he turns his face towards her and looks at her with anxious eyes.

EVA: You mustn't be so sensitive. I can't bear it. Try to control yourself. I do.
JAN: Can't you ever shut up?

Having said this, he looks even more terrified. Eva has a moment of contempt. She walks before him down the steps.

JAN: Now I forgot my jacket.

As Eva comes out into the yard, she hears the loud sound of engines, coming rapidly closer. Five trucks of heavily armed soldiers thunder past in a cloud of white dust, which drifts in over the yard.

JAN: There have been a hell of a lot of transports these past few days.

112

EVA: I didn't mean to be nasty just now. It just happened.

JAN: Don't worry love, I can answer back.

The car sways heavily and cautiously out onto the bumpy road. It rattles ominously and is grey with dirt and dust. One of the wings has fallen off.
Eva has taken off her sun glasses and her eyes are tightly closed.

EVA: It's exactly four years tomorrow since we came here. Yesterday it was a year ago since Grandad died. We mustn't forget to go to the cemetery and put some flowers on the grave.

2

A sterile landscape, with low wind-plagued woodland crossed by winding stone walls. A bumpy, dusty country road. A few farms, meagre fields, sudden views over a grey sea.
Eva lifts up the dachshund onto her knee and lays her hand over the animal's head. Jan has put on a cap with a peak that shades his eyes. He leans forward over the wheel, long and thin, his shoulders hunched.

JAN: You're right to nag me. But I was a good musician, you have to admit it. And when we were in the orchestra — those were good years. You always say I'm weak and give in. When it comes down to it, there's nothing right about me. Sometimes I just don't understand why you don't leave me.

113

EVA: You've said that a thousand times and you don't really mean it. *(Laughs)* I'm sick to death of you. You're tired of me too. Aren't you?

JAN: Yes. I'm pretty tired of you.

EVA: People shouldn't talk about feelings and things. It's such a waste of time. Oh, hell. He's got a tick. Look. Right behind his ear.

She devotes herself to the dachshund's tick. They proceed in amicable silence.

They are crossing a narrow wooden bridge. Under the bridge runs a shallow, but quite fast-moving stream. A man is standing on a large stone, fishing. Eva tells Jan to stop. She jumps from the car, leans over the railings.

EVA: Hi Philip. How's it going? Have you caught anything?

The man looks up and grins. Says something, which is drowned by the noise of the stream. Eva shouts back that she can't hear, the man makes a gesture to his throat to show that he is hoarse. Eva nods and calls that she will come down and, followed by the dog, she clambers down the steep banks of the stream. Jan remains in the car. He waves, looks at his wife, who is talking eagerly. Suddenly she is happy, smiling. Her shining red hair, her laughter; quick, impulsive gesture.

She buys a couple of salmon-trout from Philip. They discuss the price and the man laughs hoarsely. Eva fishes her large wallet from her back trouser pocket and finds a note. The deal is concluded. Philip has cut a forked stick and gives her the fish neatly hung up. Eva climbs up the

114

bank, holding the stick in her left hand. Philip says something and she turns round, he has put down his rod and comes after her. They talk together, their faces serious.

Jan can't hear anything: the stream and the wind in the trees drown their words. They nod to each other and Philip returns to his fishing.

Eva gets in the car and wraps the fish in an old newspaper. The dog jumps into the back seat.

JAN: What were you talking about?

EVA: Philip heard the radio a few hours ago. He said there was a warning for a landing. There's been fighting in the air over Ar and Hense.

JAN: They've been talking about a landing for five years now.

EVA: Well, there was a warning on the radio. Why is our damn radio never working? If only you wouldn't always repair it yourself. Can't you give it to someone who knows about radios?

JAN: It's better not to know anything.

EVA: It's better not to know anything. This escapism of yours drives me mad. And I wasn't going to nag you. Anyway, I've got some fish for dinner. See if we could get a bottle of wine.

JAN: When you stood down there talking to Philip, anyway, I was in love with you. You were so beautiful.

EVA: At a distance, you mean. *(Laughs.)*

She lays her hand against his neck. The car rattles and jumps along in a cloud of limestone dust. It has clouded

115

over ominously, and the first drops of rain are falling on the windshield.

EVA: Look, it's started to rain. What did I tell you?

The Residence is a mile or two outside town, surrounded by a well-kept park. The strawberries are delivered to the kitchen door and paid for in cash.
Eva and Jan have returned to the car and are just leaving,

when someone calls out. Mayor Jacobi has come out into the courtyard in front of the house. His big black official car has been driven round and the chauffeur (in uniform) is standing with his hand ready on the handle. Jacobi comes towards them with a smile, his hand outstretched in greeting. He is a man of about sixty with a heavy impenetrable face, a calm dark gaze, the corners of his mouth pulled down in an ironic expression. His hand is dry and hard. He is elegantly, but not pedantically, dressed.

Jacobi talks for a few minutes of the weather and wind and a record he has just acquired. He hopes that they will soon come to dinner, so that they can all play music together in the evening. His wife, who has been busy with the rose bushes, comes up and greets them amicably, if somewhat formally. Jacobi points out that his wife is now the gardener, the regular holder of this post having been called up. His wife remarks that it is becoming increasingly difficult to get servants and that things are getting worse and worse but that one must try to keep up appearances as much as possible.

A young officer with a briefcase under his arm comes quickly out of the house, gives them a friendly nod and goes over to his sports car, which is parked a bit further down the drive. Eva and Jan learn that the son of the house has been home on leave, but that he has been called back to his unit. And that he has risen in rank, in spite of his youth. The Mayor looks worried and says that something seems to be in the offing. 'But perhaps we shall be lucky this time too.' 'It's amazing the way we've been spared on our little island,' says his wife. 'This terrible Civil War.' There is a long silence and some autumn jackdaws beat their way over the oaks in the park. Mrs Jacobi has a

117

sister, who has come to stay with them as a refugee. She had the most terrible stories to tell.

The Mayor has to·leave. He shakes hands with them, thanks them for the strawberries. Eva says they are going to buy a bottle of wine, if they can find one. Jacobi laughs and wishes them luck. He gets into the black car. The chauffeur salutes, shuts the door, drives off with the Mayor. Eva and Jan take their leave of Mrs Jacobi, who repeats her husband's invitation to a little concert one evening. Even the dachshund receives an absent-minded but friendly farewell pat.

Jan and Eva leave.

The car smells of fish.

JAN: God, what a smell of fish!

EVA: You could have put the car in the shade.

JAN: It was raining when we came.

EVA: If you had put the car a bit closer to the house it would have been in the shade anyway. But you never think, do you? Sometimes I wish I had a husband who was a bit practical.

The little town is in confusion. The roads are blocked. Transport vehicles of different kinds all over the place. Heavily equipped soldiers.

Military police on fast motor-cycles, sudden groups of people with bundles and cases. Public address systems, which every now and again issue incomprehensible messages.

Jan and Eva have left the car and are pushing their way through the streets.

By a little square loaded with the attributes of war is an

118

ancient house, squeezed between two tenement buildings.
Behind a languishing garden is the entrance to an antique
shop. When the door-bell rings, a man of about sixty
emerges from a side room. He is wearing a uniform much
too large for him and he gives a worried laugh as he greets
them. His thin neck rises like the stalk of a flower from the
black hole of his collar.

LOBELIUS: You see the fancy suit they've given me?

And I haven't handled a weapon for forty years. You're lucky, Jan, with your heart condition. Tomorrow we're off. And I haven't got anyone to look after the shop. Not that it makes much difference. What can I do for you?

EVA: Have you got a bottle of wine? We can pay cash.

LOBELIUS: Well now, I have got a few bottles left. Wait here, I'll be back in a moment. Have you seen this?

Lobelius puts a little porcelain statuette on the table. A loving couple locked in a graceful but bold embrace. Lobelius touches one of the figures' chin with his finger, and from it a melody emerges (in a slightly cracked tone).
The old man goes down to the cellar to fetch the wine. Jan and Eva listen to the musical box, which fills the dark room with its brittle melody. All these objects (vain, meaningless, fragile, ugly, indispensable). They listen silently, sorrowfully.

Lobelius returns with two bottles of wine. He puts them on the counter, with an inviting gesture. One of them he has opened and from under the counter he takes three tall crystal glasses. He pours the wine and they toast each other silently. Then they drink again, greedily, in deep gulps. The melody has stopped. In here, facing the little courtyard, it is quiet.

LOBELIUS: No one knows why it still goes on. Yesterday, our radio threatened the most awful things. This morning their radio answered, congratulating us on our imminent destruction. It's all utterly incomprehensible.

120

Lobelius dries his eyes and gulps down some wine. Somewhere inside, a clock chimes in the silence.
Eva is seated in a black chair. Jan is leaning over the counter.

I feel like crying. *(Laughs.)* But I'm simply scared. And why am I scared? I'm alone with my things. Once a week Mrs Prince comes to clean. When she has finished her cleaning we have coffee and go to bed together. I don't think she'd miss me very much. But, you see, I'm afraid. Physically afraid.

EVA: This is a really lovely wine. But do you think we can afford the other bottle?

LOBELIUS: You can have it for ten. I'd give it you free if I could afford it. But I have to leave a little money with Mrs Prince to look after my things.

Eva takes out her wallet and puts down two shining silver pieces on the counter. Lobelius puts the unopened bottle of wine into a bag. They take their leave hastily and rather shyly. The old man follows them to the door. He has large boots and drags one of his feet.

LOBELIUS: One of my feet is bad. Do you think they take that sort of thing into account? Perhaps I could get some administrative job?

JAN: They take feet very seriously indeed. That I do know. We had a colleague . .

LOBELIUS: The main thing, I suppose, is to show yourself willing. I mean, if you tried with a medical certificate and all that . .

121

They take their leave once more. Lobelius locks the door after them, remains standing by the window looking out into the garden with frightened eyes.

At the cemetery is a little stand that sells flowers and wreaths. They buy a wreath of immortelles for five kronor and visit Grandfather's grave, which lies in a dark, remote corner. The grass has grown high around the stone. But the inscription is clear.

EVA: We ought to straighten it up.

JAN: What good would that do?

EVA: Perhaps not. *(Reads)* David Fredrik Egerman, born 25 August 1914. Died 18 July 1968. *God is my strength.*

They lay the wreath on the stone and depart. Some old women are busying themselves by a grave.

From the street comes the noise of heavy motor vehicles, voices on the loudspeaker and military music.

3

They come home in the afternoon. Sit in the sun by the wall of the house and eat boiled salmon-trout and drink white wine. For once the table is laid, with some autumn flowers in a cream-jug. The dachshund is under Eva's chair. The cat is on the steps. The summery buzzing of a bee.

Flushed with the wine. Jan speaks of various repairs he intends to do about the house. Eva, smiling, informs him that at last she is going to start her course in Italian. Jan wonders whether they shouldn't start their violin practice again, for an hour a day. They still have their instruments

122

and they will be going back to the orchestra as soon as the war is over, at least that's what had been agreed. Eva, who has become a little tipsy, starts saying that it was time she had a baby. That it gets more difficult to give birth every year. That she doesn't feel herself to be a woman, because she doesn't have three children. She says that they should both have themselves tested and that she is practically certain there is nothing wrong with her. That she is probably very easy to get pregnant, but that Jan must have had so many dangerous affairs while they were separated that he is incapable of having children. Jan promises her that he has been utterly faithful to her, except for that awkward occasion when she found him in bed with the opera singer. Eva decides, for her part, that he has no idea what real love is. Jan claims that he has never loved anyone but Eva. 'Yes, yourself', says Eva. 'If only you weren't so selfish.' Jan answers that he has actually decided to change character. He does believe in real and basic changes in character. He is no determinist. Faced with this grand and important word they both fall silent a moment, after which Eva says she doesn't give a damn whether Jan is a determinist or not, if only he would be a bit more thoughtful and – for instance – was capable of mending the waste pipe in the kitchen. He promises to do it the following morning. Suddenly, Eva softens. He tells her she is beautiful in this light and she thinks they have had a successful day. They leave the table without clearing away. As Eva stands over the washing-up and Jan has gone to the woodpile to chop some wood for the stove, they can see very clearly an air battle being fought in the pale evening sky. A few aircraft tumbling silently around, lit up by the evening sun. They stand silently, their heads bent back.

123

The evening is quiet, far out to sea below the horizon is heard a faint but ominous rumbling. Then everything happens very quickly.

Suddenly, from nowhere, is heard a furious, torn scream. Over the tree-tops, terribly close to them, limps a fighter aircraft, a trail of fire streaming from one wing. It brushes over the house and bores its way in through the edge of the woods, tears down the trees, bores still deeper in, breaks up. A white light and then an explosion. A rain of metal and stones. Then, red flames in the darkness of the forest.

A parachute is swaying uncertainly above them, a man suspended vulnerably from it. It moves rapidly towards the ground. (There is no wind and it does not drift, only sinks down.) The hanging man moves his legs, they can see a small white face, a pair of clutching hands. Man and parachute vanish behind the trees, just beyond the fire. A low roar, a series of explosions. The flames twist upwards in a ragged spiral.

Eva and Jan are quarrelling, panicky and frightened. She wants them to go out at once and find the poor man in the parachute. He says she is mad, it's probably one of theirs, and they could be shot down at any moment. She says he is a coward and a fool and she is going into the woods alone if he is too frightened to go with her. He is furious at her recklessness and holds her fast; she screams at him to let her go, she hits him, he releases her and she starts to run into the woods, in the direction of the fire.

He stands uncertainly for a moment, then collects an old hunting rifle from the hall. Jan has caught up with his wife and they go quickly towards the fire. The aircraft has ended up in a little clearing and set fire to a barn and a

124

dried-out tree. There are small fires on the ground and at the end of the road ploughed by the aircraft.

At the edge of the meadow they see someone moving, the pilot. He is caught up in his lines, hanging suspended in a pine and cannot get loose. His face is bloody and he is heaving convulsively. The dog is under the tree, barking excitedly. The man calls out something to Jan but his shout is choked in a gurgling sound. He beats his clenched fists against his sides, in powerless anguish. 'I'll get help,'

shouts Eva and runs off.

Jan is left alone with the dying man. He stands there helplessly, staring at the suspended, struggling figure. Looks into the eyes, wide open in anguish. The dog barks shrilly and unceasingly. The wind blows through the woods and carries the smoke in between the trees. The sunlight pierces the shadow in places, hard and yellow. 'Kill me,' screams the man, pulling up his upper lip in a grimace. He gives a rattling cough and black blood gushes from his mouth. Jan cannot bear it, he runs away as fast as he can. Behind him, he hears inarticulate screams.

When he arrives at the house, the yard in front seems to be filled with soldiers. Perhaps no more than ten or a dozen but it seems a lot. Two jeeps stand by the edge of the road. Eva is talking to an officer. The soldiers run past him towards the place of the fire. 'They were already here when I came,' says Eva in terror. The officer, an older man with a shiny fat face and watery blue eyes, looks at Jan and his gun with indifference.

OFFICER: Did you see if there were one or two of them who bailed out?

JAN: We only saw one. Didn't we? Yes, one.

OFFICER: Did you shoot the pilot?

JAN: What? Me? No. How do you mean? I ought to have killed him?

The officer gives a bored shrug and says something about why did you have your rifle with you.

Someone comes up to him and speaks in a low voice. 'Let him hang there,' says the officer. Pockets his pen and paper and walks towards the jeep.

126

OFFICER: I'd advise you to get out. We'll have them here by morning. They've dropped paratroopers only a few miles away. Try to get south, if you've got the chance.

Jan asks something but gets no answer. The two jeeps vanish beyond the stone wall into the woods.

They start packing. It is dusk but they waste no time lighting a lamp. Winter clothes, hoarded canned food, household articles, the rifle, blankets and coverlets, a pillow, the cat, the dachshund. On with boots. Matches, candles, a bottle of aquavit, plates. Jan drops three on the floor, Eva has no time to be angry. Everything in a muddle of cases and boxes, paper cartons and bags. The old car is soon loaded. No not the cat, it can always manage, but the dachshund has to come.
Now it is almost dark. The fire is still burning over there but not so violently. The sky is light and everything is absolutely still.
They emerge from the darkness. Silently and suddenly they are there, their faces blacked, heavily armed, in dirty uniforms. They drag Jan and Eva out of the car, she resists and has her face slapped. Jan receives a blow in the neck and falls headlong. They are pushed up against the wall of the house, standing in sudden terror side by side, their hands clasped above their heads. The men talk in low voices, pull out the contents of their car, invade the house. Cones of light from their torches play over the windows.

SOLDIER: You're the one who shot the pilot over there. Right?

127

JAN: I haven't shot anyone.

SOLDIER: You'll only make it worse for yourself by lying. Did you shoot the pilot?

JAN: He was dying when we got there.

SOLDIER: What are you lying for?

A hard blow over the face. Jan falls over but gets up again at once. Eva gives a small scream but is silenced.

SOLDIER: Was there an A.G. patrol here before we came?

JAN: They were here half an hour before you got here. They warned us that you were only a few miles away. They came with two jeeps, I think there were twelve or fourteen of them. They took the road down towards the sea. Didn't they, Eva? They told us to get out of here as soon as possible.

A little further off stands a man with his sub-machine gun pointed at Jan's stomach. He lights a short cigar-butt. The flame of the match lights up his blackened face.

SOLDIER: Where do you belong? Whose side are you on?

JAN: I don't belong anywhere. We're musicians.

SOLDIER: You *were* musicians. There aren't any orchestras any more. What about you?

EVA: I'm unpolitical, like my husband. We don't belong

to any party.

The soldier regards them for a moment or two. Then he turns to someone back in the darkness. Two men speak in low voices. The old car backs over the yard, creaking and shaking under its rough treatment. The floodlights are aimed at Jan and Eva by the wall. Someone comes forward with a microphone. Another produces a film camera. A third soldier moves into the circle of light. He has put a microphone round his neck and removed his helmet. He tells Jan and Eva to put their hands down, offers them cigarettes. The camera starts, the car engine hums.
Immediately between the brilliant lights, the interviewer is glimpsed as a dark cardboard shadow.

INTERVIEWER: We're making a programme for our television. We want to show audiences at home what sort of people we are liberating. We've already interviewed lots of people like yourselves. Right, let's make a start. Ladies first. Wesster, have you got the camera on the lady? What's your name?

EVA: Eva Rosenberg.

INTERVIEWER: Tell us something about yourself.

EVA: I'm twenty-eight years old. I'm first violinist in the Philharmonic Society orchestra. My husband and I have been married for seven years. We have no children. When the orchestra folded up, we moved here to the farm, which I inherited from my grandfather.

INTERVIEWER: What are your political views?

EVA: I've never bothered with politics. What is happening around me I just do not understand. Anyway, our radio's broken.

131

INTERVIEWER: So you don't care whether you live in a democracy or a dictatorship?

EVA: Hasn't the war been going on far too long for us to know which is which?

INTERVIEWER: Democracy, Mrs Rosenberg, means living on our own responsibility. Democracy is belief in mankind and the greatness of mankind. Wesster, we'll take Mr Rosenberg. All ready? What's your name?

JAN: I'm feeling sick. Do I have to? I've got a weak heart. Can my wife go and get my medicine? I'm feeling terribly sick.

His eyes wander in the harsh light, he puts his hand to his face. Then he tumbles over, lies prone on the ground, his arms under his body.

Eva bends over him and the soldier takes him by the neck and shakes him. Voice from the darkness: 'The bastard's only pretending.'

INTERVIEWER: No, he's fainted. *(To the cameraman.)* Did you get the faint? No? Probably just as well. Kill the lights.

It is pitch black. From the woods, the brief sound of firing. Violent movement in the yard. Whispered calls and running footsteps. A flashlight shines briefly and is turned off. The machine-gun fire continues. The men vanish over the stone wall, down over the hills towards the sea. The firing continues for a few minutes and then stops.

Jan sits up. Eva wanders round in the dark, at last finds the medicine. Jan swallows the capsule with difficulty.

JAN: I was so frightened. Weren't you frightened?

EVA (*wearily*): Can you get up now? Try to get up.

They stumble into the house. Jan supports himself on Eva. She lights a stump of candle, they make their way upstairs. Entwined closely together. They kick off shoes and boots, let their outer clothes fall to the floor, creep into bed and draw the coverlet over them. They hold each other tight, silently entwined, close up against each other.

She caresses his cheek, he presses his forehead against hers, pulls her tight up against him, it gives warmth.

EVA: I was thinking the whole time, what a good thing we haven't any children.

JAN: When peace comes, we'll have children.

EVA: No, we'll never have children.

She presses herself up to him and he feels that her cheek is

wet.

They hold each other, in a moment of security. For them, this is the first day of the war.

4

They are woken at dawn by a roar, which steadily gathers in strength; the house rocks, the window-panes rattle. The dog, which has slept at the end of the bed, howls in fright. They hurry out to the yard. In the grey morning mist, they see a strong glare of gun-fire over the woods. Again and again, the ground is shaken by explosions. From the sea is heard an inarticulate screaming, interspersed with heavy thuds. No one is to be seen. They are alone and the world is coming to an end.

They collect their belongings into the car, in a flurry of confused words and plans. 'Where, which direction?' 'Should we stay, should we hide in the woods?' 'What should we do?' 'Let's take the road down to the sea.' 'Shall we take the chickens with us?' 'At least they'll be something to eat?' 'Who's going to wring their necks?' 'Not me.' 'Not me either.' 'Shall I shoot them then?' 'Have you heard of anyone shooting chickens?' 'Well, for God's sake, you don't expect me to cut their heads off. It gives me a pain in the heart just to think about it.'

Jan aims his gun and shoots. A cackle, wings beating and a rain of feathers. 'I think I missed, where the hell did it go?' 'Up there on the wall.' 'No, I'm not going to shoot a chicken.' 'Leave them to live as long as they can. The eggs may always be of some use to someone.'

The car swings out through the gates and down towards the sea.

135

In the bend in the road is a tank, the barrel of its gun pointing towards the water. At the edge of the wood sits a bearded man with a radio transmitter; he stares in astonishment at the old car, which pulls up just behind the tank.

Another man emerges from the inside of the tank. He is holding a sandwich in one hand and a plastic mug of coffee in the other. Jan bows politely and retires. Trying to turn the car, he drives it into a ditch. Not a deep ditch but the damn thing is stuck. The soldier with the transmitter comes up and asks if they need help. The one with the coffee shouts something into the interior of the tank.

Eva gets out and they all exchange suitable greetings. Soon, five interested men are gathered around the capsized car. They hold a brief discussion on the best approach. A chain is brought out. The monster starts up and drives along a few yards, the car is up on the road again. They say 'goodbye' and 'thanks a lot'.

They go back the same way. The sun has risen and is shining on the red tiles on the roof. Everything looks tumbledown and fragile in the sound of gunfire. It is four in the morning. Jan holds his watch to his ear and can hear it ticking.

He sits waiting for Eva. She crosses the courtyard with a coverlet rolled up under her arm.

They drive a few miles inland. The sound continues unceasingly, like some infernal machine. A jeep has stuck in a ditch, there are soldiers standing around the vehicle. The other jeep is further up the road. The officer who interrogated them the day before is still sitting in the driver's seat, beside the driver, who has collapsed over the wheel. The sun is shining on the fat pale face of the

136

officer; his eyes have an expression of stupid surprise, his mouth is open and his fat, womanly hands are resting on his knees. Jan makes a detour to pass the jeep, driving the car out into a field where the crop stands high and unharvested. They have never seen a dead man before.

The neighbouring farm is still burning. The barn has collapsed and thick smoke is pouring from inside. Out in the yard lie the husband, wife and two children, all shot. They are wearing their night clothes.

A little further on, the road is blocked by a wrecked tank. It has a large hole in its side and emits a powerful smell. There is no one to be seen. They have no chance of getting past. Jan and Eva stand silent, as if worn out, in front of this final obstacle.

Jan reverses, turns and drives back home to the farm.

Without saying a word, they unload and put everything back in place in the kitchen and rooms.

They are sitting opposite each other at the kitchen table, the dog on Eva's knee.

JAN: The tanks are firing down by the bend now. This bloody noise. I can't stand it. I can't go on any more. I can't.

He puts his hands over his face. Eva looks out through the window, biting her lips.

She gets up and leaves the kitchen. Jan follows. She stands in the little hall, fumbling with a big sweater, which she takes off.

EVA: Can't you leave me alone, even for a minute?

She sits down beside him on the steps and takes his hand between hers. They sit in silence side by side, listening to the storm of gunfire.

JAN: Perhaps we should go down to the cellar. Don't you think it's safer there?

EVA: You go if you want. I'm not going to sit up in the dark like a rat.

Short, hard explosions are heard continuously from the tank down at the bend in the road. This sound is then drowned by ground strafing aircraft, zooming in on their targets at low altitude. Wave after wave of them. Jan turns his torn face towards Eva and says something, she shakes her head. They can no longer hear each other. The detonations have come closer and suddenly the windows in the upper part of the house are shattered and a powerful pressure wave hits the wall of the house. Jan tries to speak again. But he can produce only scattered, incoherent words.

When the firing has continued in this way for six hours (it started at dawn, at about 3.30), it begins gradually to die off and finally stops altogether. Silence.

Eva and Jan go out into the yard. A wind has begun to blow and there is a strong, acrid smell. A hen is cackling behind the woodpile. There is a rustling in the leaves of the old oak. Raindrops patter into the water barrel under the drainpipe. Somewhere, a sea-gull screams. Now they see the tank come lumbering up the road and drive into the woods, where it stops. The crew get out and approach the house. They ask for something to drink.

All the men know is that they have been recalled to base, that the enemy had landed down at Kyrkviken, but been repulsed. They add that Jan and Eva were lucky to get away with a broken window.

The evening sun paints a red pattern on the wall by the bed but leaves Eva's face in the shadow. She sits curled up in her dressing-gown, looking at Jan, who is in the middle of the floor in his pyjamas. He is standing with Eva's violin in his hands. The bow is on the table.

139

JAN: Did I ever tell you who Pampini really was? He was
an instrument maker in Vienna, a contemporary of
Beethoven, and had learned his craft in the Italian
school. He had been enrolled in the Russian army for
many years and fought against Napoleon. Then he lost a
leg and started making violins. This one he built in
1814, the same year as the Congress of Vienna. Then he
died of the cholera. I forget what year.

He tunes the instrument and lets it sound; then he takes the bow and shakes his head.

JAN: It sounds too awful. My hand's absolutely ruined. You have a try.

Eva shakes her head, with a little smile.
He puts the violin back in its case and closes the lid. It is quiet. Quiet in their house, in the woods, over the sea, quiet in the air. The sun goes out slowly behind the pines.

EVA: Come here to me.

5

A few days later they are picked up for questioning, pushed into a military truck with a crowd of people they don't know and driven to the summer restaurant.
This has been turned into the HQ of the interrogation team and the yard is full of people and vehicles.
They are shut up in a corridor-like room with nailed-over windows and a number of latrine cans along the bare walls. There are already some twenty people there. From time to time, some of them are taken out. None of them come back.
The air is stifling and smells of sour straw and perspiration. Jan is in his pyjamas; Eva has managed to get a coat on over her night-dress.
When they asked to be allowed to dress, they were told that they probably wouldn't be needing clothes very much in the future.

A man of about fifty is slumped beside Eva. He has a longish pale face and a narrow, bitter mouth; his eyes are large and black with anxiety. He is wearing gold-framed, slightly tinted glasses. His hands are very well cared-for.

OSWALD: How do you do. My name is Oswald. We met on the occasion of the charity concerts a few years ago. It was I who — I'm a teacher, and youth leader. Or was. Things don't look very good. *(Laughs bitterly.)* I've

been reported by a couple of my students. Do *you* know anything?

EVA: Not a thing. We were just taken and brought here.

OSWALD: They call it 'decontamination'. And now after this last victory, they can afford a blood sacrifice.

JAN: We're absolutely innocent, we've told them time and again.

OSWALD *(shrugging his shoulders)*: There's the vicar going out now, the old swine. They found twenty

143

paratroopers he'd been hiding in the crypt. He's not long for this life. It must be my turn now. Look at my hand shaking. That's interesting, isn't it? I mean, this business of fear.

JAN: What did you do?

OSWALD: I have a passion for the classics. Art, ethics, philosophy, politics and so on. I'm a humanist, if you don't find the word pretentious.

The door opens and Oswald's name is called. He rises with a frightened smile, makes his way through the crowd and vanishes. A fat man at the opposite wall laughs and takes out a cigarette, which he tenderly divides in two.

MAN: I know that one. He's a queer, he's been seducing schoolboys by the dozen these past three years. It's only right that they should get him, now they're having a decontamination.

JAN: What about you?

MAN: Black market. *(Grins)* There's not a bastard hasn't been buying from me. Including the bastards leading the interrogation.

JAN: Have you been inside?

MAN: Not yet. But I know how to handle it. Want a cigarette?

Eva thanks him and takes one. Jan refuses politely.
A new group of people are pushed into the room. The electric light is switched on. A guard says there will be food in an hour. Someone shouts out that the buckets ought to be emptied.
The fat man folds his arms over his chest, hunches up,

144

closes his eyes and yawns. A child screams in a piercing voice, someone is talking on and on in agitated tones. Jan rests his head against the wall and closes his eyes. Eva is smoking.

EVA: Sometimes everything seems like a long strange dream. It's not my dream, it's someone else's, that I'm forced to take part in. Nothing is properly real. It's all made up. What do you think will happen when the

145

person who has dreamed us wakes up and is ashamed of his dream?

Eva and Jan Rosenberg are called out. They emerge into the hall, which has a red tiled floor. Officials move to and fro. Some young guards with sub-machine guns. A raw cold, blended with terror.

Jan gasps again and again for breath and yawns. Eva smiles uncertainly at someone who is looking at her. 'Do you know you've got odd shoes on?' *Eva suddenly asks. Jan looks down, sees that she is right and gives her a quick frightened smile.* 'We're not going to get out of this,' *he says. Eva doesn't answer. There is a large ugly brown clock on the wall. It says quarter past six.*

A door opens and they are escorted to the interrogation room, which is square and fairly large. The windows are nailed up and there are powerful electric lights in the ceiling. At one table is a secretary (a small man correctly dressed in civilian clothes and with an indifferent, almost bored, expression). The door is guarded. The interrogation officer, a thin man in uniform with the rank of captain, is standing talking to a round-shouldered, blond-haired youth, whose uniform jacket is unbuttoned. Heaps of files and a mass of papers on the table.

The floor is dirty. Here and there we glimpse what might be a bloodstain.

Jan and Eva are seated on their respective chairs.

The interrogation officer sits down at the table and looks at a paper, which is provided by the blond man with the unbuttoned jacket.

INT. OFFICER: We have reason to believe that you have

been collaborating with the enemy. You will not be judged unheard. The most serious evidence, of course, is Mrs Rosenberg's television interview, in which you entirely endorsed the political views of the enemy. Have you anything to say?

EVA: It's not true.
INT. OFFICER: Not true? We do in fact have a recording of the interview, would you care to hear it?

A tape-recorder starts, a loudspeaker begins to rasp. An indistinct female voice. 'I wish your troops victory. We have suffered too long under oppression, been too long bereft of freedom. We have longed for liberation like those thirsting in the desert.'

EVA: That's not my voice. They've used my face and put another voice on it. I never said a word of all that.

The round-shouldered blond man goes up to her and takes her by the hair.

BLOND MAN: Now you're going to tell the truth, otherwise both you and your husband will suffer. Have you got that? No one wants to hurt you unnecessarily, but we don't like lies in this place.
JAN: Don't try to deny you said it, Eva. Much better tell the truth.

The interrogation officer stares at Jan in open contempt. Then he turns to the secretary and whispers something to him.

EVA: It was silly of me. I confess.
INT. OFFICER: And what form did your collaboration take, apart from that?
JAN: We never collaborated.
INT. OFFICER: Then how do you explain the fact that the paratroopers who liquidated the entire civilian population within an area of more than one square mile – how do you explain that *they spared you and you alone*? That you are the only survivors out of more

than three hundred people and that your house was left undamaged.

EVA: If we gave the interview we were to be spared. We refused at first, then we gave in. What could we do?

INT. OFFICER: Take Mrs Rosenberg out for the moment. We wish to talk to the man alone.

The round-shouldered one pulls Eva up from her chair and throws her towards the door. She recovers her balance and stands for a moment leaning forward, but is kicked from behind and falls to the ground. She is lifted up and put outside the door.

A large room with a parquet floor and pictures with summer motifs on the walls. Bathing youths and girls. Matrons with small naked children. Elderly gentlemen in white summer suits.

She turns round and sees Oswald half-sitting on the floor. He is without his glasses, his black eyes are surrounded by bruises, his mouth is swollen and bleeding, his clothes torn and bloody. He seems hardly to know where he is.

A scream is heard from inside the room. It is Jan screaming, loud and high. Someone is speaking in an angry voice.

On the wall a green luxuriant tree, beneath it a loving couple with a luncheon basket. Over by the door, a broken juke-box and a colourful advertisement for some make of cigarette.

The door is opened and Jan is thrown in, he tumbles round on the floor.

Almost simultaneously, two men who have received similar treatment are lifted or thrown into the room. The second of them has been given a cigarette, which he smokes

149

silently; time and again, his eyes fill with tears.
Through a tapestried door comes a doctor, with two
assistants. He is lean, elderly and has large false teeth and
thick glasses; his forehead is red and he smells of alcohol.

DOCTOR: *(To Jan.)* Can you stand on your feet. H'm?
   Yes, well, that's all right, isn't it. Nothing wrong with
   you. You still seem to have your arms and legs. *(To
   Oswald.)* You look a bit of a mess. Lift him up. No,

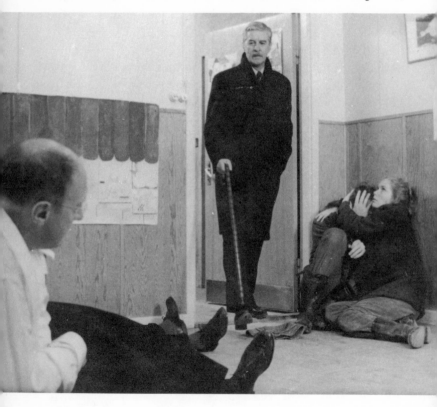

we'll have to take him to the hospital. *(To the man who is screaming.)* Shut up a minute, will you? What's wrong with you? Ah, they've pulled your shoulder out of joint. Come over here and we'll put you straight.

They hold the man fast and the doctor pulls him backwards, upwards. The patient lets out a bellow.

DOCTOR: Don't play tennis for the next few weeks. Here's some tablets to deaden the pain, you'll think you're in heaven. And what's wrong with the lady? Nothing? All the better. Would you care for a cigarette? I just got them from a black marketeer I had to patch up. What about that one over there? Is he asleep? No? Then you'd better get him out into the ambulance truck, for God's sake. He can't just lie here.

The doctor scratches his forehead and looks around, as if noticing the room for the first time.

DOCTOR: This was where the Sailing Club used to meet. I used to come here a lot. During the autumn Regatta. Have you had any food? No? I'm afraid you'll have to excuse us. We've only just moved in and we haven't got properly organised yet. I'll tell them to send you something in. Good evening.

He marches out with his assistants. Somewhere a radio can be heard. People move up and down the corridors. The very lack of sound insulation creates a silence around the three who remain and isolates them. The man with the shoulder is a journalist on the local newspaper. A premature bulletin had come in announcing the success of the landing. The paper had been reset and they had produced a front page welcoming the liberators. In spite of everything, the man seemed to have been humanely treated. They had released him as soon as he began to scream in earnest. They seemed embarrassed and somewhat unused to the job.

According to the journalist, this business of having a doctor is something new, it has never been done before. Jan tells how he has taken a tremendous beating from the round-shouldered man and his assistant. The interrogation officer had gone out of the room while this was happening. They said he was being punished for making a bad television programme.

A woman comes in with a large tray and three plates of soup. She glowers at the prisoners and leaves as soon as she can.

A few hours later they are awakened and taken out into the courtyard.

It is almost dark and the air is frosty. They are pushed together with a group of about fifty other people. A company of men is drawn up along one wall of the restaurant. A pile of sand-bags has been stacked up against the kitchen wall.

Two big searchlights have been mounted on a wooden platform. Screams and the tramping of feet. A man in jeans and a white shirt is dragged into the yard, resisting with all his strength.

His is lashed to a thick wooden pole in front of the sand-bags. A hood is pulled down over his face. The officer in command gives an order. The man screams inside his hood. Then silence.

152

Mayor Jacobi comes into the courtyard. He walks with difficulty, supporting himself on a cane. He is in uniform, with the rank of colonel. He places himself in the glare of the searchlights, in front of the condemned man, facing the prisoners. His face looks older and swollen in the sharp light. His heavy head is sunk between his shoulders and his eyes are red-rimmed from lack of sleep.

JACOBI: This man is condemned to death. He has

153

collaborated with the enemy and caused us heavy losses. At the order of the government, he is to be pardoned and his death sentence commuted to life imprisonment. You others who are standing here will also receive more lenient sentences than you could otherwise have expected. You will receive humane and just treatment. Those of you who are tried before a court will have a defence counsel. Some of you will be set free immediately and given transport to your home districts. Get the

prisoners in line.

*The officer gives orders. The mob of prisoners is pushed
forward and lined up against the wall, the searchlights
aimed directly at their faces. Jacobi walks down the line,
pointing with his cane.*
*Each person who is to be released has a white slip of paper
fastened to his chest.*
*Jacobi recognises them. He stops and regards them with a
trace of a smile. Then he gives orders that the two
prisoners should be taken at once to his office and wait
there under guard. He moves on.*
*A wooden ramp in the darkness. A doorway and a step.
The light is turned on in a large office. Another door.
Jacobi's room.*
*A guard sits down by the door. He has a bag of sweets and
from time to time pops one into his mouth.*

EVA: Can we sit down?
GUARD: Like hell you can sit down. If Jacobi sees you
    sitting down he'll half kill you and me too. Congratu-
    lations, anyway. You're in for a right time. I wouldn't
    want to be in your shoes, I really wouldn't. Not that
    I've ever seen anything myself, but I've heard stories. We
    thought that sort of thing was all over. That they'd gone
    in for other methods. You know, more modern.
    Psychological. But then yesterday. That poor bloody
    vicar. Jacobi gave him a going over that lasted three
    hours. I didn't see him afterwards, but those who did
    said it made them want to throw up.

Footsteps, slow and halting, are heard on the steps. Jacobi

155

enters. He is breathing heavily after the effort, his legs seem to be causing him difficulty. He tells the guard to wait outside for further orders. He opens the door to an inner room and asks Jan and Eva to come inside.

This is a small drawing room. Comfortable furniture, curtains in the windows, a large bookshelf, a record player, great piles of records, lamps that give a restful light, a carpet on the floor. He asks them to sit down, goes to a cupboard, takes out brandy and glasses, pours some for them.

JACOBI: I heard about the famous interview. It was a fake from beginning to end, we knew that. But we had to set an example and I couldn't stop them arresting you. There's no need to worry any more. Justice has been done. I told them to be careful, I said Jan Rosenberg had a weak heart and that absolutely nothing was to happen. How do you feel?

JAN: All right, thank you.

JACOBI: No serious wounds, anyway, as far as I can see. And Eva here only had a bit of a shock. I forbade them to touch you. I trust I was obeyed.

EVA: Their behaviour was . . . almost correct.

JACOBI: Well, that's always something. Cheers, anyway. I hope we'll meet some other day when we have a bit more time to talk. I imagine you will want to get home as fast as possible. I'll get a car for you, so you don't have to take the transport.

He limps off to the outer office and rings various numbers. Curses the lack of organisation, asks brusquely to speak to the officer of the day, asks the latter where the hell his

156

driver is, rings a new number, says that things are going to be very different as from Monday, at last finds the right person and asks in a surprisingly courteous tone for a car to be placed at his disposal.

He shakes their hands and wishes them a pleasant ride. Roars at the guard on the steps to go with the car and see that Mr and Mrs Rosenberg get home all right.

This is not at all what the guard was expecting and he stares suspiciously at Jan and Eva when they have got into the car. He takes his place beside the driver, but cannot help turning round from time to time during the journey to look at the two passengers.

It is an icy cold autumn night and they have been given a blanket to wrap themselves in.

They sit close up together, half asleep.

6

A few weeks later a cease-fire is signed. The autumn days are cold and it rains almost unceasingly, from time to time a snow-squall comes in from the sea. The dead have been removed and buried. People start drifting back from their hiding places further inland.

Some delayed autumn ploughing is started here and there. Jan and Eva are planting potatoes. The field is large, the job heavy. They work in sullen silence.

JAN: That's all I'm doing, I've had enough. It's all so pointless anyway. You carry on if you like.

Eva continues determinedly. Jan stays, watching her work. He is furious.

157

JAN: Now you're being a martyr. Slaving away, being self-righteous. But my God, you're filled with hate.

Eva doesn't answer, but her back tautens.

JAN: It's odd. As long as there was a war on, at least we were fairly decent to each other. And now the worst threat is over we can't bear the sight of each other. Can you explain that? It's 10 o'clock, I'm going in to hear the news.

EVA: You sit there in front of the radio. That suits me. I won't have to look at you.

JAN: Jacobi gave us the radio so we can listen to the news. He said it's important.

EVA: If it's all that important, you'd better not stand here talking.

JAN: You said yourself yesterday, after Jacobi had gone, that he was a good person to have as a friend.

EVA: I never said that.

JAN: Yes, you did. But you were so drunk, you must have forgotten half the things you said.

Jan, raging, has begun to help Eva with her work. They remain silent, soaked through by the icy drizzle.

EVA: I'll tell Jacobi not to come here again. Philip had a word with me. He says it could cause trouble for us, if anything happened.

JAN: Is Philip going to decide what guests we have in our home? That is really the stupidest thing I ever heard.

EVA: Jacobi comes here and gives us presents. He sits here all evening sometimes, drinking.

158

JAN: He's always been very decent to us. Don't let's pay any attention to all the talk. We don't know anything.

EVA: Well, at least you don't have to be so obsequious to him.

JAN: What about you then?

EVA: I'm not obsequious.

JAN: That's exactly what you are. You run around crawling to him.

EVA: Say I crawl to him and I'll hit you.

JAN: Crawl, crawl, crawl, crawl, crawl . . .

Eva stares at her husband in fury. Then her face relaxes in sudden boredom. She has soil on her cheek and her hair lies heavy and wet on her forehead.

EVA: When peace comes, we'll leave each other. God it'll be marvellous to get away from you and your idiotic childishness. It's not only you whose life has been ruined. There happen to be other people in this world than you. Don't stand there grinning. You're not as bloody remarkable as you think.

She hits him as hard as she can and falls over. Starts crying. Jan sits on the wheelbarrow with the potato sack. It is beginning to get dark near the woods. Some sea-gulls are strutting in the field, like stiff small ghosts.

JAN: We can't go on like this. It's utterly useless and we both know it. I'm sorry.

EVA *(angrily)*: You're always very quick to say you're sorry. Do you mean it, or is it just something that slips out of your mouth?

159

JAN: We've said everything that can be said and a bit more. Can't we be friends?

EVA: Yes.

She gets up and brushes off the earth with her hand. He helps her, a little lamely. She takes his head between her dirty hands and bends over him.

It is dark, the paraffin lamp is whispering gently (there is paraffin to buy again). The little transistor radio is on and the Rosenbergs are going to bed. The old dachshund starts barking. Shortly afterwards a car is heard and there is a knock on the door. Eva goes downstairs to open it.

Jacobi is standing out in the darkness, at the foot of the steps. Bare-headed, dressed in civilian clothes, with a shiny black raincoat. His shoes are muddy, as if he had walked a long way on wet roads.

He has a couple of objects wrapped in newspaper under his arm.

The big black car is down on the road. In the front seat can be glimpsed a uniformed chauffeur.

JACOBI: Sorry to come so late. Am I disturbing you? I was out for a walk and really intended going straight home. Then I saw you had your light on and thought I might as well look in. If I'm not disturbing you. Perhaps you were just going to bed?

EVA: We were just listening to a Mahler symphony.

JACOBI: I don't want to come in with muddy shoes. Do you think Jan has a pair of slippers he can lend me? Can you put my shoes by the stove? They're absolutely soaked.

Eva goes before him out into the kitchen and lights the paraffin lamp. Takes Jacobi's shoes and puts them by the stove. Jacobi sits down at the kitchen table, leaning forward, his big palms pressed against the oilcloth.

EVA: If you don't mind, we'll sit in the kitchen. It's so cold in the other rooms.

JACOBI *(Calling)*: Jan Rosenberg, where the hell are you? You've got company.

Jan comes down the stairs, greets Jacobi cordially and asks how things are.

JACOBI: Bad. I've just had a letter from my wife. She's in Switzerland.

EVA: Not bad news, I hope?

JACOBI: Why should there be bad news? Good God, no. Everything's going splendidly. We'll have real peace within the half-year. There's a cease-fire all the way, and both parties — well, you've got the radio. You know.

EVA: I meant your wife. No bad news from your wife.

JACOBI: I brought something to drink with me. A bottle of Renault Carte Noir. What do you say? Have you got some glasses? Eva darling, you're more beautiful every day. Can't you leave this half-wit you're married to and come to me instead? I'm much better, I promise you. In every way. I don't think I'm quite sober. No, I can't be. I had half a bottle of whisky before I went for my walk. In the beginning, you know, Eva, in the beginning it didn't affect me at all. But now. You know, Eva, I think it's the smell. When people are frightened they sweat and when the boys take their clothes off they're often

161

wet through with it. It smells.

EVA: Do you use torture?

Silence. Jan stares at his wife. Jacobi raises his head and looks at his glass, which he revolves between his fingers.

JACOBI: I brought a present for you, Jan. It's a very smart present, but I'm giving it to you, I inherited it from an uncle. A first edition of Dvorak's Trio in E flat major. One day we can play it together, all three of us. I've got a present for Eva too. Here, take it. I hope it's the right size. It's an old family heirloom.

His present is a ring, with diamonds surrounded by rosettes in a strange pattern.

EVA: You mustn't give us so much.

JACOBI: Haven't you received me in your house and given me your friendship? What was I going to say?

He sinks into a heavy silence. Eva shows Jan her ring and he shows her the score. Then they look a little anxiously at Jacobi, whose mind is obviously elsewhere. There is a knock on the door. Jan goes and opens it. It is Philip. Jan doesn't let him in, but Philip can see Jacobi's back through the open door. Philip asks to borrow a gallon of paraffin. He gets it and disappears into the darkness and rain.

JACOBI: Who was that?

EVA: No one in particular. Just a good friend. He looks in from time to time. He wanted a gallon of paraffin. And after all, you gave us a whole barrel.

162

JACOBI: I ought to give up smoking. Those people, you know, believe in the importance of what they're doing. They're driven by a terrible idealism.

EVA: And aren't you?

JACOBI: Eva doesn't like me tonight. If I asked her for a kiss, she'd say she didn't dare for your sake, Jan. But you wouldn't object to Eva giving me a kiss?

JAN *(laughing)*: You'll have to ask her yourself.

Jacobi gets up and goes round the table, leans over and looks at her in desperation.

JACOBI: Well, will you give me a kiss?

Eva pulls his head down towards her, and kisses him on the mouth. He sinks down on one knee and cups his hand over one of her breasts. She lets it happen.

EVA: You're nice and we like you, but you put us in a difficult situation by coming here all the time.

Jacobi laughs. Gets up and stands on the floor, supporting himself against a chair.

JACOBI: This business of being an artist. Is it all it's cracked up to be? Does it free you from all your obligations? You're wrong. It's no longer possible to refer everyone simply to the colossal sensitivity of your soul. Say what you like, do what you like, okay. But take the risks. You don't want me here. I understand. So you've told me.

EVA: Don't be stupid. You're drunk and you're talking

163

nonsense.

JACOBI: I saw you just got frightened. If I sniff at your arm-pits now they'll smell of fear. It's a pity I like you. That you've come to be my friends in the twilight of the world. Otherwise I'd send you to a labour camp. Are you afraid, Jan Rosenberg? Are you an artist or a sack?

JAN: I'm a sack. But sit down and let's talk about something else. We could listen to a little music, for instance.

JACOBI: The holy freedom of art, the holy gutlessness of art. I will pay no attention to Eva's remarkable contribution to the conversation. Now let's listen. *(Sings).* I'm going out for a piss.

Eva and Jan try to sober up, but can't.
They are enclosed in a dream, from which they try in vain to waken. It just becomes heavier to breathe. The dream closes inexorably in on them.

EVA: God, if only I could sober up. I've never been so drunk.

JAN: We've got to get him out. That was a nasty thing with Philip.

After a fairly long while, Jacobi returns. He now seems balanced, sober, calm and dignified.

JACOBI: Forgive me Jan, my dear friend, but I went out in your slippers. I've got them dirty.

He takes the slippers off. Fills his pipe with care and lights it, asks for a glass of water, which he gulps down in one go.

164

He lifts the dachshund up on his knee and strokes its head.
A long stillness.

JACOBI: The woods are full of people. They're waiting
   for the right moment. I've sometimes wondered what
   they'll do to me. I'm ready to admit the idea frightens
   me. There's no reason why they should torture me, I
   don't have any secrets to tell them. But perhaps they
   will still want to put me through it.

Silence. Jan is sitting on the wood basket. Eva leans her
head in her hand and looks out into the darkness.

JACOBI: Did I frighten you? *(Laughs.)* I'm sorry, I was
   only joking. Do you think I would be stupid enough to
   come here, if I wasn't safe? We have patrols throughout
   this entire sector. And our clean-up has been very
   effective. *(Yawns.)* No, there's no danger. Not for you,
   not for me.

He pours out brandy and tastes it, slowly and with
pleasure. Stillness once more.

JACOBI: I think I have built up a debt by what I have
   had to do this past year. And I know that I shall be
   punished. Do you believe in crime and punishment?
EVA: No, I don't believe in that.
JACOBI: There are people who are seized by a devotion
   to their executioners, I've seen it myself. The discovery,
   the revelation, the punishment, these have a rare power
   of attraction. I'm boring you.
JAN: No, of course not. Go on.

165

JACOBI: I only think when I speak. And for the most part I keep silent, as I'm alone. So — no thoughts. May I ask you something. Do you experience each other? Don't look so damned stupid. I mean it. Are you just two ideas circulating round each other and taking hold of each other and talking to each other? Or are you living people who touch each other the whole time?

Jacobi empties his glass, gets up and puts down the dachshund on the table. He goes over to Eva and begs her to feel with her hands his head, his forehead, his eyes, his nose and mouth. He unbuttons his shirt and places her hand against his chest. Then he turns to Jan and takes him and his hands. Head bent, he grips their hands and holds them fast for a long minute.

JACOBI: When they stank of fear, I could understand them. But not enough to stop me. I have only experienced human nearness a few times. Always in connection with pain. Is it the same for you?

EVA: It's not like that for us.

Jacobi nods gravely, as if a theory of his has been confirmed, and he goes out into the hall, staggering slightly. He stands there looking out through the small window. His shadow is dimly visible in the very early dawn.

JACOBI: You can't speak about it. It all seems so artificial. Almost indecent. No, there's nothing to say. Nowhere to hide. No excuses or invasions. Only a great guilt and a great fear. And the smell.

It begins to snow. In absolute stillness. The paraffin lamp has gone out and the small rooms are filled with chiaroscuro. Jan sleeps, exhausted by emotion and heavy with cognac. His head rests in his arms. He is seated asleep at the kitchen table. Eva goes around picking things up, clearing away.

JACOBI: It's snowing.

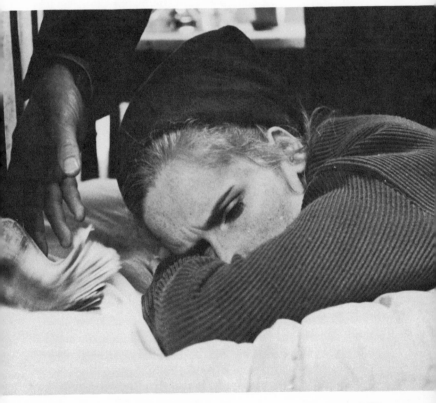

Eva answers something and continues making her quiet movements in different directions. Jacobi watches her.

EVA: I think you should go home.
JACOBI: I felt this change of weather in my bad leg. Eva, come here a moment. Come here and I'll give you something.

But Eva does not go to him. She has gone into the adjoining room (a small square bedroom with ancient furniture and a gold-framed mirror on the wall).
She has lain down on a convertible sofa along one wall, one arm under her head, her hand playing with some strands of hair. She shuts her eyes, immobile, closed in on herself. Jacobi goes over to the table by the window, pulls a wad of notes from his pocket and puts them on the table.

JACOBI: Twenty-three thousand. I want you to have them.
EVA: I don't want your money.
JACOBI: Don't be stupid. You'll just be inheriting it from me.

He goes to pick up the brandy bottle and the glass. She watches him, then turns her head to the wall. After a few seconds he is back. He sits down in a low wicker chair by the wall.

JACOBI: I was home at my son's place yesterday, he's on leave. He has a little boy of nineteen months. The kid was just going to bed, his father was feeding him

168

formula out of a large cup. He sat like a safe little baby monkey, cuddled up in his father's great body. By the time he had had enough he was almost asleep.

Eva turns her head and looks at him.

JACOBI: My wife had had a miscarriage. It's many years ago now. The day before Whitsun I picked her up at the hospital and we took the boat out to our summer place. It was a warm sunny day, in May. We walked together in the woods, by the paths we usually took. Everything was absolutely still and all the birds were singing. We hardly spoke to each other, but we were closer to each other than ever before or since.

Eva says nothing, watching him steadily.

JACOBI: My mother died a few years ago. She was old and had a bad heart. One Sunday morning they rang and said she was very ill. I went home to see her. When I came into the living-room the doctor met me. I said 'Can I go into my mother for a while' and he said, 'Your mother has just passed away'. Then I was in with her for an hour, I just sat looking at her. She had a little piece of plaster on her forefinger. Sometimes I thought she was still breathing.

Eva watches him in silence.

JACOBI: No, it's not much that gets through. All we hear is the cry. If only it was conviction. Do you know why I took this job? I was given a choice. And I was afraid of

169

being sent to the front.

Eva watches him steadily.

JACOBI: Do you have any regrets?
EVA: No.

He stretches out his hand in appeal. She pretends not to see it, sits up, smooths her hair.

EVA: Sometimes I get frightened when I think about it. So I don't think about it. I've never been unfaithful to Jan before.

He bends over her to kiss her, but she turns her head away. 'Not here' she says in a low voice. She takes him by the hand, takes him out of the house, over the yard, where the new snow is forming grey-white patches in the light of the dawn.
They go into the greenhouse and find a place on some old sacks.
Jan, drunk and half-asleep, wanders to and fro in the house. He calls for Eva, in a low, unhappy voice. He is tortured by tooth ache. He finds some sort of headache powder, which he pours into himself with a slug of brandy. His anxiety increases steadily. On the table in the bedroom he finds the money. He stands there with the wad of notes in his hand and a heavy nausea in the pit of his stomach. Then he puts the money in his pocket. Goes out onto the steps, sees the footprints in the snow, doesn't know what to do; he goes inside again, sits down on a chair in the kitchen, finishes the brandy, whining to himself from time

170

*to time like a sick dog. He goes upstairs, rinses his face in
cold water, shivers, puts on an extra sweater, looks out
through the window, lies down on the bed, pulls the cover
over himself, shivers so much that his teeth grind. Whispers
'Eva, Eva, Eva' in a complaining voice. Says: 'That swine
Jacobi'. Says: 'I've only got myself to blame.'*
*He grows hot and feverish, throws off the covers and gets
up. Looks at the time, it is 4:30.*
*He sits on the steps with his head in his hands. 'This hellish
toothache.' Presses his forefinger against his cheek.*
*It has grown lighter and the snow has given way to rain.
Eva catches sight of him in the doorway to the kitchen. He
turns round hastily and looks at her anxiously. He stops
Jacobi and asks him to stay in the hall.*

JAN: Alright, how is it going to be? I've known the
whole time. But when you've got the nerve to — right in
front of my nose. All right, that's how it is. Is Eva going
to move in with you? Is she?

EVA: Can't you be quiet?

JAN: Do you love each other?

EVA: Can't you keep quiet. Jan, please, don't say
anything.

JAN: I've only got myself to blame. I've thought about
that all morning. It's right that Eva should leave me.

*He stands in the doorway, holding his hands behind his
back and supporting himself against the doorpost. Eva
takes off her coat. A few minutes of complete silence.
Jacobi stands at the outer door, looking out through the
small window.*

171

JACOBI: I wonder where my car's got to.

Jacobi goes out onto the steps, lights a cigarette. Jan shakes his head. Eva fills a saucepan with water and puts it on the stove. Jacobi says goodbye, giving them a slightly confused nod. Jan does not look at him. Eva says goodbye, in a low voice. Jacobi goes over the gravel, hunched up slightly against the rain. Jan sits on a chair in the kitchen, the dachshund presses up against his leg.

JAN: What was the money for?
EVA: He wanted us to hide it for him.

She has put out cups, butter, bread and jam.

JAN: He might as well have got something hot inside him before he left.

Eva, about to fetch the saucepan, suddenly stops. Jan too turns his eyes towards the window. Jacobi is standing beyond the wall down by the road, speaking to some men (some of them in oilskins like fishermen, others in leather jackets, one of them in a short sheepskin coat, all of them armed; they are about eight altogether, one or two of them middle aged, the others very young, about seventeen). Jacobi is addressing himself the whole time to one of them, speaking calmly, smoking. The man looks towards the house. It is Philip. They turn back, come up towards the house. Philip and Jacobi enter the hall. The others sit down outside. The two go into the little bedroom.
Philip greets Jan and Eva briefly, shuts the door. After waiting a few minutes, Jan tries to go out onto the steps,

172

but is pushed back inside.

More waiting. It is raining. The flames flicker in the fire. Somewhere, a clock is ticking. Philip opens the door and tells Jan and Eva to come in. Jacobi is sitting on the sofa. He still has his coat on and is smoking. His face is hollow and thin, his shoulders are hunched; he looks small and wretched. He clears his throat. Speaks in a grey, harsh voice.

JACOBI: We've been discussing things a bit. Philip says I can buy myself free, since the organisation is in need of ready cash. Idealism obviously isn't everything and even the men of the Resistance have to be paid. I must therefore beg you, Eva my dear, to loan me back the money I gave you last night. This embarrasses me, but it is necessary. Would you be good enough to give it to Philip?

EVA: Jan's got it.

JAN: I don't know anything about any money.

Philip sighs and narrows his red-rimmed eyes, he is obviously very tired. Jacobi begins to shake. With some difficulty, he lights a new cigarette. Jan looks at the floor. Eva has sat down.

JACOBI: So you didn't take the money?

JAN: I don't know what you're talking about.

PHILIP *(yawning)*: Tell your husband to bring out the money, if he's got any.

JAN: I don't understand, what money are you talking about?

173

JACOBI: He's hidden the money.

EVA: If you've hidden the money, you've got to get it. It's not your money.

JAN: We've got two hundred in a tin box in the kitchen.

PHILIP *(greyly):* We'd better look around a bit.

He goes yawning out onto the steps, where he is seen talking to his men. They push Jan, Eva and Jacobi out into the yard. Then the search begins. It involves tearing out and breaking the household equipment and utensils, throwing furniture through windows, ripping up sofas and chairs, tearing off wallpaper, slaughtering pictures. Everything is done quickly and methodically. Eva's and Jan's instruments come dancing through the window. Master Pampini's superb creation from 1814 is crushed against the gravel of the yard. Jan's violin remains in its case but has split lengthwise. He takes it up, then throws it away, it lands with a strange sound on the stone step. A quarter of an hour, half an hour passes.

Someone has found their stock of canned foods, comes out on the steps with it all in a big case; another steals Jan's boots, a third empties the rabbit cages. Jacobi has sat down on a garden chair, now he has almost vanished into his black overcoat; he is shivering and breathing into his hands, his face as hollow as that of a dying man. Jan and Eva stand a few yards apart from each other. Philip comes out onto the steps with the two hundred, throws the tin box on the ground, puts the money into his pocket, says something to his second-in-command, who passes the word on. They all come out of the house. One of the men (a sixteen-year-old from the neighbouring farm, who survived the massacre) gets into Jan's car and starts it, backs it up

174

against the wall of the house, gets out, fires a few shots into the petrol tank, which explodes. In a moment, the entire old house is on fire.
Philip turns to Jacobi and says something.

JACOBI: Yes, I know.
PHILIP: You know what you are charged with?
JACOBI: Yes.
PHILIP: And you also know what we have to do with

you?

JACOBI: Yes, I think I know.

Jacobi's teeth are rattling and his eyes wandering. He has got up and is standing opposite Philip. The grey dawn grows lighter, there is a hard, icy wind. Philip waves to Jan.

PHILIP: Come here. You've had some difficulty making up your mind. Now I'm giving you some medicine.

He reaches towards Jan with his pistol and makes a gesture towards Jacobi. At the same time, Jan has a weapon aimed at his face. There is no turning back. Eva has run backwards, her arms pressed between her legs. The fire roars and provides heat. Jacobi and Jan exchange a few words. The men stand waiting. Jan drops the weapon to the ground and shakes his head, but is immediately afraid and picks it up again.

Philip says to him to hurry up, they can't stand there all day. Jan fires and Jacobi takes a step backwards, clutching his hand to his stomach. Then he bends forwards. Jan fires another shot and Jacobi falls to the ground. He begins to cry and scream. Jan goes closer and fires at his head. Jacobi rolls round and flails his legs in the gravel, tries to get up. One of the men fires a few shots at the back of his head. Then Jacobi lies still.

Philip takes the weapon and issues orders. The men depart down the road, carrying with them Jan's and Eva's last possessions. The house is burning furiously, the roof falls in and a tall pillar of flame rises upwards. The dog, its back broken, lies at the bottom of the steps.

The men turn off from the road and vanish behind the

176

hills. Eva goes into the greenhouse and sits down in a corner. Slowly, Jan follows her. The fire is reflected in the panes of glass, colouring everything in a mild yellow. Slowly, it becomes warm. They sit for a long while in silence.

EVA: You took the money?
JAN: Yes. I did.
EVA: Where did you hide it?
JAN: I didn't hide it.
EVA: Where have you got it?
JAN: Here in my pocket.

7

In the time that follows, they live like terrified animals in the depths of the greenhouse, which they try to arrange as best they can with the rest of their belongings. They sleep a great deal, rolled up in a variety of garments. They eat turnips, swedes, potatoes, which they boil over an open fire. Often, they search the ruins of their house. From time to time they find something that can be used. The little transistor radio, some books, a saucepan, a chair, the old mirror in its golden frame. Otherwise, they devote their days to collecting supplies for the winter, and fuel (there is a rusty old iron stove in the greenhouse).
They hardly talk to each other. Eva weeps violently from time to time. One day Jan gets furious and tells her to stop. She goes on crying, still more desperately. He hits her in the face. From then on, she keeps her tears to herself.
The radio provides scanty reports on the Civil War,

177

*difficult to hear and increasingly confused. The armistice
has been broken by both sides, but the real fighting has
stopped and given way to a menacing calm. Both sides
accuse each other of bestial deeds of violence, particularly
against the civilian population.
And then this is what happens.*

*One day in late autumn, they have been in the woods
looking for mushrooms. Returning, they find that a
stranger has found his way to the greenhouse. He is sitting
hunched up in front of the stove, a young boy in the
uniform of the paratroopers. (A very torn and dirty
uniform.) His sub-machine gun is lying by his side. When
Jan opens the door, the weapon is seized and aimed at
him. The man's face is thin and childlike, the eyes are
scared. When he sees that they are unarmed, he calms
down a bit – but is still very much on his guard. Eva asks
if he would like something to eat, he says that he is
hungry, they give him a few potatoes, which he devours.
One of his hands is bound up in a dirty bandage and two
of his fingers are sticking straight out, stiffly.
He is running a temperature, his lips are cracked, his eyes
over-bright. He asks if they have anything to kill the pain,
his hand hurts so much, he has been bitten by a dog. Eva
gives him some aspirin and asks if she can look at the
wound. He himself has some bandages and disinfectant.
While Eva bandages the boy's wound, Jan sits on the bed,
his hands in his pockets.*

JAN: Did you defect?

The boy does not answer at once but he nods.

178

JAN: What's your name?

JOHAN: Johan.

JAN: Have you been in hiding for long?

JOHAN: A few weeks. There are people everywhere who've got out, they're just drifting around, plundering whatever they can find. If only I could find the way to Hammars. Is it far from here?

JAN: What do you want in Hammars?

JOHAN: I'm not saying. I've got to get there before Tuesday.

Everything is quiet for a few minutes, the wind rushes through the pipe to the stove and the rain beats faintly on the glass roof.

EVA: Aren't you going to lie down for a bit?

The boy grows suddenly suspicious, shakes his head and pulls his weapon close to him.

EVA: Why did you run away?

JOHAN: Everything seems sick. That's why they all talk so much. I wonder if anyone really knows why the war keeps going on.

He coughs and looks sick. Jan reaches him a cup of hot water, which he has heated on the stove.

JOHAN: There were several of us left at the same time. I don't know where the others went. Three of them got caught almost at once. I haven't slept for several days. It doesn't hurt so much any more.

179

He stares in confusion at Jan and Eva, his head drops on his chest, he recovers at once with a tortured grimace, mutters 'I have to keep awake'.

JOHAN *(smiles)*: If I shot you both I could sleep. As it is I daren't sleep. And I can't go away, because my head's all dizzy.

JAN: Say why you have to go to Hammars on Tuesday.

JOHAN: What? To Hammars? Did I say that? I can't

shoot you either, you've been decent to me. So far, I haven't managed to kill anyone.

He falls asleep again, this time heavily. Jan bends forward and takes away his weapon.

EVA: Let him alone. Let him sleep. Let him alone.

This she says in a whining voice. Jan doesn't answer, he sits for a moment or two thinking. Then he gets up and kicks the boy awake. Tells the boy to go with him. Johan begins to swear and cry. Jan tells him to keep calm. They vanish in the misty drizzle on the road down to the sea. Eva listens for a sound. She goes out into the yard, hears the sound of the sea and some jackdaws circling over the edge of the woods. She starts to run along the road to the shore, then stops out of breath, listening anxiously.
When she gets back to the greenhouse, Jan is already there. He is sitting, as previously, on the bed, his hands buried in his pockets, his expression one of indifference.

EVA: What did you do with him?
JAN: There's a fishing boat leaves from Hammars at dawn on Tuesday. People trying to get over to the neutral zone. He heard it from a friend, who had paid to get on board. He was killed the same day.
EVA: What did you do with the boy?
JAN: I took his equipment off him. His shoes are worth having, mine are finished.

Jan sorts through the soldier's pack, the rifle and ammunition lie beside him. Together with some tools and a knife.

EVA: What did you do with him?

Jan turns towards her, hits her. She does not cry, just lowers her head.

JAN: We're packing. We've got to be at Hammars before dawn.

EVA: I'm not coming.

JAN: It'll be simpler if you stay.

He moves busily to and fro in the confined space. Gathering together his few possessions and stowing them in the pack. Eva puts a saucepan on the stoves and looks in their food store.

EVA: We'd better have something to eat before we go.

JAN: I mustn't forget the radio. But it's almost finished.

He turns the knob. Through a loud crackling, emerges a slow, well articulated voice.

RADIO: — the right to live as free citizens of a free country — this bloody feud between brothers — for nine years — innumerable sacrifices — these silent heroes — the flower of our youth. The time has come for the final battle — will be terrible and without mercy. This is the wish of the enemy — our desire for reconciliation — the ultimate weapon — where we have previously hesitated, we must now act with firmness — this appalling weapon, but in the long run — impossible.

The noise drowns the grinding, elderly voice. Jan puts the

182

radio in his coat pocket. Then puts on Johan's shoes, winds a scarf round his neck. Eva has collected their blankets and put on all she possesses in the way of clothes. Jan checks the sub-machine gun and loads it.

They leave, dragging their heavy baggage.

They go as fast as they can, through the falling dusk. There is already ice along the shore and the sea is like black ink. A red ball of sun hangs over the woods. An icy wind blows from the north.

They turn off inland and pass two burned farms that have been abandoned.

They reach the shore at Hammars well before dawn. The sea has cut deep in among the limestone rocks, chiselling out great primaeval sculptures, like faces turned to the horizon.

EVA: Jacobi gave me a feeling of safety. I knew it was wrong. That he was old and tired and a coward. He

promised to help us in all sorts of ways. He said that when the war was over he would be a person to reckon with. I knew, I was practically certain that he was lying. That he was just a scared little man doing a dirty job that no one else would take.

JAN: Don't talk about it.

EVA: What's it going to be like if we can never talk to each other any more?

The boat appears, a dark fleck on the still grey morning sea. People begin to creep forth from holes and caves, moving frozen and clumsily like heavy wingless insects.

The boat scrapes against the rocks on the shore and Philip gets out. He pulls the passengers on board, one after another, helping some of them with their cases and bags. There are seven persons in all, four men and three women. Jan asks to talk to Philip. They walk together along the shore. Jan asks if he and Eva can come along. Says that the young man who paid for his place has been killed. Philip answers that it will cost money. Jan says he has money and asks how much is required. Philip says that the others have all paid ten thousand each. Jan finds this reasonable and gives Philip the wad of notes. Philip laughs and asks where he had hidden it. Jan says he had had it on him. Philip laughs even more.

Jan asks why Philip is leaving. Philip looks out over the sea and the unwilling ice-grey light of morning.

PHILIP: It's piss, all of it. I don't know. Nothing.

Philip helps Eva aboard. She is almost apathetic. The passengers greet each other without friendliness but have

185

to crowd tightly together. One woman is very ill.
Philip has some difficulty in getting the boat out, as it is heavily loaded. No one is prepared to help him, they are all afraid of being left behind. They push and struggle with oars and poles.
High up on the shore, a heavy rumbling is heard and a tank appears. It stops on the edge of the cliff. The passengers, in terror, start trying to clamber out. They are stopped by a huge loudspeaker voice, resounding over their heads, over the sea, over the deserted stony shore.

THE TANK: We are letting you go, because you are a disgrace to your country. We do not want even your dead bodies. You have forfeited, for all future time, the right to a country. Hurry away, the air will be cleaner when you are gone. We know who you are. We know your names. We know your crimes. Sometime barrister Ernst Bergman and his wife, who has worked for both sides and betrayed and sold his friends. Sometime surgeon Peter Arman and his wife, who has deserted a children's hospital with five hundred patients. Sometime fisherman Philip Olsson, who has killed for both sides, and profited from transporting defectors. Sometime paratrooper Johan Egerman, deserter. Sometime engineer Paul Andersson and his wife, who has provided false information and received payment for it. Go now and go quickly. You are not worthy even of our contempt.

Jan suddenly runs forward, screaming.

JAN: What about us then? Have you forgotten us? Jan

and Eva Rosenberg. Why not call out our names? Don't we exist any more? Why won't you answer? What have we done?

He stumbles among the rocks, screaming. Someone grabs at him but he pulls free and continues upwards.
The tank makes no reply. The sea soughs and swells. The engine starts. And the great dark machine disappears in reverse. Soon it is out of sight.

187

They have been at sea only a few hours when the sick woman dies. The body is heaved over the side. The wind has dropped and the water is almost still. The radio, which is suddenly heard very clearly, plays dance music. We can assume that it is a foreign station. Jan and Eva are together but say very little.

Early the following morning, the engine stops and the boat drifts in the calm. They take turns at the oars. They are all still in good heart. At about one o'clock in the afternoon, a shadow like that of a giant fish is glimpsed under the boat, moving slowly on the same course. After a while an antenna protrudes, followed by the whole body. It is a submarine. Some men appear on deck, for a moment a gun is aimed in their direction, then the men vanish and the submarine dives. Once again, the sea is deserted.

On the third day their water is finished and the food runs out. It has blown up slightly. The men are incapable of rowing. The boat is off course. The sky is grey and cloudy and it is rather cold.
Eva tells Jan of a dream from which she has just awakened. They are close together, face to face.

EVA: I had a strange dream, it was absolutely real. I was walking along a very beautiful street. On one side were white, open houses, with arches and pillars. On the other side was a lovely park. Under the big trees by the street ran cold dark-green water. I came to a high wall, that was over grown with roses. Then an aircraft came, roaring down and set fire to the roses. They burned with a clear flame and there was nothing particularly terrible

188

about it, because it was so beautiful. I stood with my
face against the green-water and I could see the burning
roses. I had a baby in my arms. It was our daughter, she
was only about six months old, and she was clutching
my necklace and pressing her face to mine. I could feel
her wet open mouth against my cheek. I knew the
whole time that I ought to understand something
important that someone had said, but I had forgotten
what it was. I pressed the baby close to me and I could

feel that she was heavy and wet and smelled good, as if she had just had her bath. And then you came on the other side of the street and I thought that you would be able to tell me about the important thing that I had forgotten.

The fourth day. Strong sunlight from a cloudless sky, no wind. The boat has drifted into a mass of dead men (several hundred), floating in their life jackets. The passengers set to the oars, to get the boat out. It is an arduous job.
The dead men stick to the sides of the boat and the oars slip on their shapeless bodies. The stench is difficult to bear.

In the night, after the fourth day, the sky is lit up by a strong glare, lasting for several seconds. Then darkness again and an absolute silence. Some of the passengers are now very sick and have become apathetic.
The fifth day. The radio is so faint that Jan has to hold it to his ear to hear anything. He then reports what he has heard: bombs have been dropped by both sides. The Western District and the North-Eastern District. A line from the fishing grounds to (name incomprehensible). A list of unfamiliar place-names. A voice warns against the water, which is polluted; the wind, which is from the south-west, means that precautions should be taken immediately. Also, a belt of rain is moving over the eastern parts of the country. This rain is highly dangerous. All foodstuffs in the affected areas should be destroyed and not used in any circumstances.
The sixth day. They sleep a lot, waking up from time to

190

*time and talking to each other. The radio is completely
silent. Some of the people in the boat are already dead.
Large, strangely shaped clouds drift over the sky.*

JAN: I was wondering what it said in those letters we
   wrote to each other during the summer tour. Whether it
   said 'My hand in yours' or 'Your hand in mine'.
EVA: It said 'My hand in yours'.

*On the seventh day a storm blows up, and there is a heavy
rain. The survivors slake their thirst with the poisoned
water.*